FIRST LIG

FIRST LIGHT

Encountering Edward Said
and the Late-Style Jewish Prophetic
in the New Diaspora

MARC H. ELLIS

Bridwell Press
Southern Methodist University
Dallas, Texas

Bridwell Press is the professional publishing arm
of the Bridwell Library (SMU Libraries
and Perkins School of Theology).

Cover art by Marc H. Ellis
Interior design by Alicia Beebe

Printed in the United States of America

ISBN: 978-1-957946-05-4 (hard cover)
ISBN: 978-1-957946-10-8 (paperback)
ISBN: 978-1-957946-04-7 (ebook)
ISBN: 978-1-957946-11-5 (OA ebook)

for

Edward Said

whom I encountered once again

on Yom Kippur

and

Aaron and Isaiah

my lifelong companions

Writing isn't just telling stories.
It's exactly the opposite.
It's the telling of a story, and the absence of the story.
It's telling everything at once.
It's telling a story through its absence.

MARGUERITE DURAS

The world is gone, I must carry you.

PAUL CELAN

In life, absolute justice eludes us; only ongoing negotiations, conducted in a myriad of ways, remain. If everything in life is negotiated, so too is the prophetic.

CONTENTS

ACKNOWLEDGMENTS

I would like to thank Professor Susanne Scholz for her support over the years and for her work in bringing my manuscript to the attention of Bridwell Press.

Thanks also to Anthony Elia, Director, and the J.S. Bridwell Foundation Endowed Librarian at the Bridwell Library at the Perkins School of Theology, his staff, and Alicia Beebe for shepherding my manuscript into a publishable form.

Finally, I offer a special thanks to Dr. Carolina Dionco for her advice and diligent creative work on making my book come alive with my photos and paintings and, in a larger sense, helping me to collect my lifetime's work into a flourishing archival collection.

SHABBAT LIGHT

Is first light different on Shabbat
My own service
Daily
Magnified?
Voice waves reach me
Low tide walk
Candlelight sky
How dark the sky is
As far as the eye can see
Opening
Golden light!
My window
Intense
Brief
Low tide invitation
I accept
The day after
Already a memory

PREFACE

MORE THAN FIFTY YEARS AGO, as a sophomore, sitting in Richard Rubenstein's classroom, having never thought of writing a book, I remember his advice – when you write a book, always write the preface last. I did not give his suggestion much thought until I began writing books myself. Then it made sense.

For Rubenstein, and now for me, a book is an exploration of sorts, a journey into the unknown, rather than explaining what is already understood. Once you understand what is to be written, the journey is over.

Though this has applied to the previous books I have written, this book fits Rubenstein's "preface first" suggestion best. The pages that follow are an unusual combination of journaling for forty or so days in the second half of 2021, without a thought of publication, and a series of meditations written in fits and starts as my journal was unfolding, with additions a year later. Here they come together, complimenting each other, building on similar themes but working through in different ways within an extended timeframe.

Constant throughout are my thoughts on the Jewish prophetic in its evolving nature and with its relevance for Jews of Conscience and those of conscience outside the Jewish fold. What can we say about the prophetic in our time? Though there are abiding themes in the Jewish prophetic imagination and beyond, the prophetic is constantly evolving. The prophetic has a developed essence that evolves over time and in different contexts and, for that reason, no matter its consistency, the prophetic is also contextual.

The prophetic moves with the times. While this has always been the case, the way we look at the prophetic at times can become static. When this occurs the prophetic, as it is understood, and the prophetic tradition itself, must be scrutinized and interrogated. If simply accepted as handed down or as it was conceptualized in a certain era, the prophetic, so explosive in its origins, loses its power. The central prophetic thrust for justice is reduced to slogans.

In the twenty-first century, the challenge to the Jewish prophetic is extreme by way of the Holocaust and the establishment of the state of Israel, the two formative events in Jewish history we inherit. The power of these events, in their destructiveness and hope, has reoriented and disoriented contemporary Jewish life. That Jews could suffer mass death, form a state, and cleanse and occupy the Palestinian people in such a short, almost contiguous time, was bound to challenge Jews to the core. That challenge continues as I write.

When Jews undergo such powerful formative events in close succession, the entirety of the Jewish tradition is mobilized, especially the prophetic, the indigenous of Jewish. For centuries the prophetic was downplayed in the Jewish world, as most Jews lived as part of a weak diaspora and too often under oppressive conditions. During this time, especially in Europe, the Jewish prophetic turned outward to critique unjust power primarily in non-Jewish societies. After the Holocaust and the founding of the state of Israel, for the first time in centuries, if not a thousand and more years, the Jewish prophetic, responding to the exigencies and abuse of Jewish empowerment, unexpectedly arrived home.

In these pages, I explore the coming home of the Jewish prophetic which has split the Jewish world into opposing camps. The direction of Jewish history is at stake and a Jewish civil war has erupted. The stakes? What it means to be Jewish after the Holocaust and after Israel – and what Israel has done and is doing to the Palestinian people.

If the stakes themselves aren't high enough, the prophetic invoked by Jews of Conscience, remarkable in its explosive strength, is also weakened. After the Holocaust, the Jewish prophetic cannot call upon God, at least in a public way. For the Holocaust has made the claim of God almost impossible. As well, Jews are entangled in empire empowerment in Israel and the United States. After the Holocaust exposed in a dramatic way the dangers of weakness, can Jews, choosing an ethical framework to embrace others, afford to challenge their own empowerment?

How does the late Palestinian intellectual, Edward Said, figure into this equation? In many ways and with me personally, Said was a towering figure who argued for Palestinian rights and freedom while serving as a bridge to the Jewish and broader world. During his life, and now two decades after his passing, Said continues to pose a challenge to Jewish history and the Jewish prophetic itself.

In these pages I explore the prophetic and Said's continuing journey with me and other Jews as a way of thinking through the stakes involved in contemporary Jewish history. For the Jewish prophetic, indigenous to Jewish life, is, at the same time, the root of the global prophetic. My claim is that the strength or weakness of the Jewish prophetic has a profound, perhaps decisive, effect on the global prophetic.

There are many twists and turns in this journey and my encounter with Said as it leads up to and manifests itself on Yom Kippur, the Jewish holy day of confession and judgment. In my journal, I employ my unexpected encounter with Said on Yom Kippur as a way of charting the dangers and possibilities of present-day Jewish life and its future. In the meditations that follow my journal, I probe what it means for Jews of Conscience, already in exile, to practice exile to its fullest. I trace Said's understanding of "late style," the theme of his last and unfinished book. Said applied his concept of late style primarily to great musicians in their final works, where what was expected of them, the continuity of their famous style, changed radically. In turn, I apply late style to the Jewish prophetic – what I have come to name the Late-Style Jewish Prophetic. In my mind, the Late-Style Jewish Prophetic is the reappearance and coming home of the Jewish prophetic as it undergoes its own deconstruction and re-emergence.

My meditations further explore the terrain of exile and how Jews of Conscience will fare in what I call the New Diaspora. The New Diaspora is the gathering of exiles from around the world and it is where, rather than the Jewish community, Jews of Conscience will find their voice and come to embody the Jewish prophetic in its evolving form. Speaking and embodying the Late-Style Jewish Prophetic in the New Diaspora will face many challenges, among them the reality that the Jewish prophetic can no longer call on God and where justice, at least as a full-scale proposition, is out of reach. I explore an underlying but related theme as to what is going on behind the obvious, when the indigenous, but restricted prophetic banner, is held high by Jews. Is it the case that Jews of Conscience, as they find their voice and embody the Late-Style Jewish Prophetic in the New Diaspora are protecting and saving the prophetic for another day?

Where these explorations lead and what they might mean for Jews and the world, is the subject of the pages that follow.

My considerations of the contemporary Jewish prophetic as they were written and as they are presented here are in process.

I have avoided adding explanations or footnotes as they would alter the course of my reflections and, in a way, solidify what represents a flow of conscience that remains open-ended. As I enter the seventieth year of life, my writing should be read as an exploration rather than a definitive statement. It should be read as my take on the Jewish prophetic rather than as a scholarly consensus. Too often, the scholarly community uses other people's writing as a way of controlling whatever others might think or say about the views the author presents. What results is sometimes stunning but again, too often, is a way of hiding one's views, as if consensus is the only way forward. I also break ranks by including my photos and paintings to accompany my words. This is my way of approaching the prophetic which has accompanied and haunted me throughout my life.

My approach has always been within and outside the scholarly community, at least as it presents itself to the world. There are those who will argue with my exploration or even push it beyond where I journey. That is as it should be. What I present is a lifetime of thought and commitment, my voice with others, but in the end, I take responsibility for it all. In addition, the readings I introduce in my reflections are readily available in books and online, as are the backgrounds of the people I encounter on these pages. To characterize each with accompanying references and notes would interrupt the flow of my thought and distort how I came to write what follows.

Thinking back now, in my seventieth year of life, I consider my writing here as my love letter to the prophetic.

My hope is that you, the reader, will find this approach to be an opening for you to discover and deepen part of your own prophetic journey.

PART ONE

Encountering Edward Said on Yom Kippur

FIRST LIGHT

AUGUST 1

Chapel of Love arrival. Cruise ship lights my walk. With the low tide dark, the ship's lights are beautiful. But I also know the junk these ships carry and jettison in the ocean.

As in life, I ask: Is beauty ever free of our surrounding junk?

Thinking of the body. Intimacy. Love. Justice. Everything they are. And aren't.

August muggy. The Chapel is buggy. Signs of life.

Empty tomb? Aside from Christian romanticism. What is there but to keep on?

"The pandemic of the unvaccinated." Our emergency years. Endless.

The sky opens as I write. Pastel orange, blue. Pretty.

Minute by minute we live. And die. With beauty and what surrounds it.

FIRST LIGHT

What I'm good at it. What I'm not.

The color of one's skin. The world as it is.

Those who have/not.

"Mutiny from stern to bow."

The next steps that do/not come. What to do when they do/not arrive?

Still running on (almost) empty.

August days. Mornings, too.

AUGUST 2

Dark as I journeyed to my beachside Chapel of Love. Dark now as I write.

Not much on my mind. As life comes and goes.

Muggy day. Slight breeze.

A deepening sense of gratitude that I found this daily ritual.

Painting yesterday. Though mostly going through the motions. Of. Sometimes that's what we have.

AUGUST 4

Waking late – 5:20! – but quickly out to the beach. To find it rained overnight. Cooling.

Almost like the first days of our Cape Canaveral Fall. Hope this continues as August rolls.

Dreams last night. A bus I had to catch heading out before I board. Anxiety dream. Haven't been many lately. Do I have a dream cycle?

Yesterday I finished Walter Benjamin's *Arcades Project*. 1,000 plus pages.

Has too much been made of Benjamin? Too little?

Benjamin's fascinating view of history. In the making. Looking back he finds the future already arrived.

How to break history's continuity? Should we?

The Jewish struggle – Benjamin's struggle – for the universal. Fails.

How it fails is the important thing. For Jews. For others.

After all, the covenant is at stake.

Deontologizing. An important Jewish/Other Nations playground. Gymnastics. Parallel bars? Uneven bars?

Without the sense of being set apart. Whether true or not. There is no Jewish thought. No Jewish insurgency.

What being set apart means. For this or that time. Is the (always) contested (Jewish) issue.

Being Set Apart. Its general location? Jewish Civil War.

Today's Set Apart Civil War battlefield: Holocaust/Israel.

Set Apart Civil War skirmishes on the Left: Intersectionality; Interfaith Solidarity; Anti-Zionism; Renewed Jewish Diasporaism.

Heavy surf this morning. Birds singing in the back of my Chapel.

Where are my ravens? I'm missing them. Are they taking an August vacation?

AUGUST 5

Up too early, painting. Now in my Chapel of Love. Windy. Coolish.

Are storms brewing? So they say. So far, so good this hurricane season. We shall see.

Lower-back issue – I had it before. Three years ago it erupted one night, then settled down. I'm better at handling it now.

Will the Olympics ever end? Simone Biles made her return. She's even more marketable now – physical excellence and mental health issues, that combination, strikes several chords in the American psyche.

On the public stage. Rising and falling. Money to be made. Symbolic statements, too. Why not cash in and have something to say. To those without a home?

Wheels keep turning. Moderation in all things?

Thinking as I walk: "Conscience – with history factored in."

Whose history? Particular histories clash. Conscience negotiated? Conscience. Isn't a blank slate.

Waiting all day yesterday for a UPS package. Another negotiation.

Looking through my bar mitzvah photos yesterday – October 9, 1965. Long time ago. Lots of Jewish history since. We made it big. And lost our ethical compass in the process.

Has ethical Jewish history come to an end in my lifetime?

I've been sitting cross-legged in the evening – but lost my morning prayer. Sometimes sitting/prayer go hand in hand. Other times not.

My prayer cycle is eclectic. Private devotions only.

Side Chapels. Of Love.

A guardian raven appears. Elijah!

The sky opens. Dark blue clouds above. Scattered orange on the horizon. More ravens.

Negotiated life.

Reading Benjamin yesterday: "The prophet has turned away from the future: he perceives the contours of the future in the fading light of the past as it sinks before him into the night of times."

AUGUST 6

In my Chapel of Love. Tide trending high but walkable. Sky opening slowly. Weather still great for August.

Dull head. Do I need a vacation? It's difficult to make a case considering my location. Nonetheless, a change of place might be good. Except for the pandemic, variants and all.

So it has to be. Inner turning. Toward?

How many times can a person turn. During the day, week, months, years. Life?

Perennial philosophy. Foundational theology. Essence. Bad Boy terminology.

Listening to the waves. Sounds underneath and around my Chapel – cats, raccoons, snakes, birds.

Turtles, too. Do turtles speak?

Not a raven in sight.

Thinking of Benjamin, a Nazi-era suicide. He couldn't continue.

Where were Elijah's ravens? Sometimes they arrive too late.

Elijah's ravens. When they appear. In the nick of time. When they don't.

Afternoon. Shabbat approaching.

I lie on the couch in my living room. For thirty minutes or so my eyes are fixed on a bookcase. My books have traveled high. And low. Some of my paintings lean against the bookcase on the floor. More of my paintings are above the top shelf. Just stacked there. Waiting for?

There are seashells I gathered from the beach and a painted tea kettle – ceramic – I brought back from my backpacking journey through Europe in 1973.

Behind my paintings are more books, including a wonderful complete edition of Mark Rothko's paintings. He was the real deal.

Should I frame my paintings? I have room on my walls for only a few. If I decide to frame them, should I choose the ones to frame, or should others choose for me? Perhaps my paintings will live one day in another home. What would they mean to someone else? What do they mean to me?

On the wall behind the bookcase there are flowers in a vase painted by my father, a print by Robert Marx whom I collect, and a painting by my grandmother – a small island illumined by moonlight.

Generations of (totally) amateur painters. I never thought I'd join in.

I wonder what it all means – the books in the bookcase included. Since ten days or so ago something happened to me. I'm not sure what it was. The something wasn't an event. Just an unnamed experience, in retrospect. Which now seems to be a release, a return, a separation or a completion. A wall? All rolled up in one.

Life accumulation. Danger ahead. Or possibility.

Should I worry if I don't return. To?

I'm not sure I can return. Even if it is best to. If it is possible, should I?

Since I've never known an Other life.

AUGUST 8

In my wet Chapel of Love. Rain last night. Muggy and buggy. But the sky is pretty. Dark light arriving. Like yesterday, big dark clouds, an orange glow beneath them.

Yesterday, reading and painting. An afternoon stroll on the beach. Low tide nice.

After my beach stroll, I read an account of the French woman who guided Benjamin and a few others across the border into Spain. She recalled Benjamin's heavy briefcase and labored breathing. She wondered if he would be able to make the long trek.

Benjamin and the others made it. She learned about his suicide the following day. The Spanish authorities were prepared to send Benjamin and the others back to France. Perhaps because of his suicide, though, the authorities let the others go. On their way, as was Benjamin, to America.

America hasn't – only – been empire. America has – also – been refuge.

Random thought: Jesus didn't argue his case from a safe zone. Neither did Paul. Or the prophets.

They were untenured. Untethered?

Memory: It is winter. I'm in New York City sitting in a basement with homeless men waiting for their meal. I'm "managing" the men.

Catholic Worker, 1975. Remembering the smells. The camaraderie, fights, despair. Yet it all felt right. Where I was supposed to be. A few days later, Dorothy Day told me – in a friendly way – it was time to be on my way.

"Marc, you are a thinker," she said. "You have learned what you need to learn here."

Reading of Benjamin's last days. Riveting. Sad.

Still a dull head. Anxiety dreams last night. A bus I needed to board was about to leave as I checked my hotel room for items I left behind. Was I left behind? I woke up before the verdict.

Hoping for a calm Sunday. Sometimes ahead isn't ahead. Or behind.

Tenured Jewish thought. Tenured Christianity.

Jewish thought on the run. Walter Benjamin. Hannah Arendt.

Christianity among the poor. Dorothy Day. My conversations with a saint. To be.

Does dissent within empire. Enable empire?

The (inclusive) landscape of empire.

Tethered Jewish. Tethered Christian.

Revisiting the (theological life) lessons of Tetherball.

Later at home, thinking about Benjamin. He (almost) escaped. But feeling that the contents of his heavy briefcase were safe and refusing to fall into the hands of the Nazis, Benjamin called it a life. Can you blame him?

On Dorothy Day, I knew her when she thought the saint business was a way of boxing her in. And considering the piety around the process now, she wasn't wrong.

Regarding Tetherball, which as a kid, when we were forced to play it in school, I hated. But this morning, musing on empire and religious insurgency, I think I missed the lesson Tetherball teaches. Which is, whatever our viewpoints, if we're gathered around the same tethered ball connected to the same pole. You can hit and hit without the pole moving. The trajectory of the ball is limited. Score is kept; wins and losses noted. When you return the next day, though, the game location remains the same.

Tetherball theology. Tetherball liturgy. Tetherball prophetic?

American Academy of Tetherball Religion. Society of Biblical Tetherball.

AUGUST 9

Muggy in my Chapel of Love. Has August finally arrived?

Low tide first light. Beautiful. How to describe the skies I enjoy.

Tomorrow a rendezvous with my new Parkinson's Doc. With great news to report. My month-long revival. 40 day and nights?

Yesterday reading a long review of the new bio of Edward Said. I doubt, though, I'll get the book, me the reader of biographies. But I knew Said and my encounters with him are more defining to me than his life story. Or writings.

Thus, reading the review occasioned a sadness. That I would never encounter Said again. Except through memory.

Another round of thinking about what drew Said to me – since he initiated our first and other encounters. I have written about this – his draw was, I think, about my religiosity. A religiosity he could, at least, approach.

Yesterday I was thinking that another attraction was Said's curiosity. About someone he thought was Somebody. But who wasn't recognized by any Somebody he knew. As Someone!

So Said was curious about my relative obscurity. A Limelighter himself, did he also crave the time before he was known and branded as "Said?"

Another line: Said loved cosmopolitan Jews. He found in the major capitals of empire. At empire institutions. He couldn't figure me out. Was I or was I not a cosmopolitan Jew? If so, why was he always bumping into me at (un)empire places? If not, why? And how could he relate to a Jew. Who was. And wasn't?

Said loved. What didn't fit. Since Said didn't fit, he carved out his own place. There wasn't another place like it. Anywhere! I didn't fit but hadn't carved out my own place like him. What gives?

Memories of those committed famed folks I encountered at various times in my life. Grateful for it. Yes.

Off I go. Out of my Chapel.

Another "Remembering Said" morning!

Home now.

Notes on my encounters with Edward Said:

1. Letter of introduction from him – late 1980s.

2. Invitation from him to small gathering in Paris – 1990s.

3. At various venues: Chicago, Boston, Waco, Ottawa, Jerusalem, Others – 1990s, early 2000s.

4. Future project – A one-act play. Edward Said, though deceased, pays a visit to me in my Cape home. Not a ghost but as if he was here, alive, in flesh and blood. We sit at my all-purpose dining room table – where I eat, write, read and paint. We chat about life, our

> encounters, Israel-Palestine and the world as it was and is today. He is a comforting presence, listening. But he also has questions. He's curious: What is a Jew like me doing where I am? Our conversation continues. About life, exile. What it means to be Jewish, Palestinian. What it means to leave the scene. The conversation is back and forth – parts serious, parts humorous. At the end, we say goodbye and embrace. I am in tears.

The play awaits a title and a playwright.

AUGUST 10

In my Chapel of Love. A low tide, beautiful sky, walk. It's a bit muggy – we're heading toward mid-August.

Yesterday was a Said Remembrance Day. Triggered, as they are, by this or that. Melancholy meaningful. There will be more ahead.

Strange, at least to others, Said and I never talked about the Middle East. Instead, we discussed personalities that crossed Said's path or mine. Included: My Jewishness. Life's beauty. Life's absurdity.

When we met in Waco, Texas – what a surprise! We discussed Baptist life. That I had a home in Waco. That I was living in Waco. That I was teaching at a conservative Baptist university. Said couldn't wrap his mind around it.

Marc in Waco. No way!

Said had difficulty imagining me living somewhere in particular. For Said, I was a person constantly on the move. Said's sense of the Jewish prophetic?

"I can't imagine you living anywhere, Marc," he said.

I wondered if this great and famous cosmopolitan thinker thought I wrote and spoke during the day, traveled by horseback and slept in a tent at night.

Then Said offered: "Marc, I think of you as an itinerant Jewish prophet."

You can imagine the silence that filled the lunchroom where we were conversing. I was stunned. What to say?

Another side of Said. A charmer. It was real, though. I had to explain to him. The facts of my life.

Boyish Said, His salty language. An elite from birth. Famous. He wanted to prove he was a man of the people.

So when we went to the hotel restaurant after his university lecture, Said insisted on ordering our drinks. And, though I thought it untoward for him to serve me, Said insisted on retrieving our beers from the bar.

I could go on and on. But the sky is opening. I feel like laughing. Out loud.

Picture this: Said in my Chapel of Love! Imagining his response to my paintings!

At my journey's end the past is present. As if it all was just beginning.

AUGUST 12

In my Chapel of Love. Dark sky. An array of stars shining. Light breeze. Low tide. The place I want to be.

My recent early Parkinson's diagnosis returns. Yesterday coming home, my legs felt heavy. After my triumphant announcement weeks before of returning to a daily walk. I seem to be back in the saddle. Was someone praying for me?

What we fear will happen. What we fear will return.

Memory energy. My Said days exhausted me. Not nostalgia, though. I don't seek a reprise of my public life. It was all good. At least some of it. Trauma, too. I wasn't, really, a limelighter.

Life's trapdoors. All of a sudden. You fall through.

When you find yourself on the bottom, get up. If you land on your feet when you fall, count your lucky stars.

Trapdoor Theology.

What I chose. What chose me. The indigenous Jewish prophetic. Open doors. Closed.

My teacher, Richard Rubenstein, warned me that the Jewish establishment would get me. Through intermediaries. True!

I heard his warning and continued on.

Better to have remained silent? Since to the silence we return. What accolades you receive don't add up to much.

Mostly you're used by others. For their upgrades. Where the upgraded end up is beyond me.

The UN report on climate. New York Governor Cuomo's exit. Biden's Infrastructure 1 passed through. Infrastructure 2?

My Chapel is backlit by the new massive cruise ships docking at the port behind it. Empty as they all are. Will life ever return to pre-pandemic (junk) normal?

Painting yesterday. A large canvas. I need to go bigger still. A challenge.

Off I go. Still dark. Is the sunrise delayed?

AUGUST 13

These Fallen Flowers

I fell today in my Chapel of Love

I stood right up and walked

On my way home

I found flowers on the beach

A pink rose

A red chrysanthemum

After my fall

They fell

Tonight I sit cross-legged JuBu

As I did

Once upon a time

Again

AUGUST 14

Shabbat. In my Chapel of Love.

Anxious after my fall yesterday. iPhone flashlight on when I arrive and when I leave. Navigating the stairs. A new security protocol.

Pretty, mixed-color, sky. Low tide, muggy. The beach is almost deserted.

Dreams last night. At a small conference, hanging with a couple and their young daughter. When I was about to leave, James Cone was introduced to speak. It was a surprise to me that he was there and when I looked around the room, I saw James on the side, sitting alone. Quite content he was. As if in a state of meditation. He wasn't young or old. Thin. He appeared to me like those icon portrayals of modern saints. I marveled at the scene.

Yes, I did. Travel Jewish. With James Cone. When he was fiery. Before he left our earth and before he settled in.

Lately, I realized that iconic figures are experienced differently by folks. Depending on the context of time and journey.

My encounters with Edward Said and James Cone. So different!

What matters to me. What matters beyond me.

What's gained in history. What's lost. Individual history. Collective history. The connections.

Strange visitations I have. A few nights ago Richard Rubenstein appeared in my dreams. Somewhat like Cone in demeanor. Altered.

Iconic figures. Their different shades.

Perhaps we should all be framed as icons. Our better angels.

I wonder if my past is being transfigured. Outside of my control. In my dreams. Healing?

Remembering the fallen flowers I found on the beach after I fell.

My fear of falling. Lest I become "unrecognizable to myself."

Painting on Shabbat. Silent prayer.

Minding the stairs as I depart the Chapel. The sky opening.

Afternoon. Reading the letters of Leonard Bernstein.

It's September 15, 1959. Bernstein is in the Soviet Union. After a meeting with Boris Pasternak, Pasternak writes to Bernstein in his halting but beautiful English. About art: "So must be art. We must will its produced impression, long, and pine for it. Art must leave us love-stricken, and sorrow overcome, like a deep-felt parting or separation. Art is the language of greatness, greatness is disclosure, its sight, its tragic and suffering being exposed to view."

AUGUST 15

Morning, 6:20. In my Chapel of Love. With light arriving. After a beautiful morning yesterday. Stunning. What will the next hour bring?

Flashlight on as I entered my Chapel. Observing safety protocols.

Tropical Storm Fred is safely away from us. Now Grace appears. Hope she steers far away from. Everyone.

Haiti – earthquake. Awful. Spared the worse?

Afghanistan in turmoil. Kabul surrounded by the Taliban.

Biden's honeymoon is over. Afghanistan might be the end of things. I'm thinking politically here. Midterm elections on the horizon.

Interesting how Kamala Harris has disappeared. Already. Another political liability.

Dreams last night but no encounters I remember. The intensity of it all. My normal.

Where does our intensity go. When we're in full stride? When we're in decline? After our demise?

Still reading the letters of Leonard Bernstein. Intensity plus. At the end he fell apart.

Remembering a conversation I had with Dan Berrigan about "Lenny." Berrigan could be generous. Also cutting. Berrigan's sarcasm.

My time with Berrigan. Quite something. My first encounter with a priest.

In Tallahassee (1974). Then at the Catholic Worker (1974-75). At Maryknoll (1980s). Vanguard mentality. Arcane Discipline. A Catholic one-off for sure.

The tapestry he brought me from Colombia.

Years earlier. Dinner at his Jesuit residence. What was I, a Jew, to do with Berrigan?

Watching Berrigan say Mass in the Catholic Worker soup-line kitchen, East 1st Street. Dorothy is in the front row. Radio Jimmy is in the back of the room in his bathrobe. That opens too wide and too often. As he roams to and fro. Muttering. Music blaring from the street. The threat of drunken/drugged violence. Occasional bricks through the window.

Home now, listening to the news. Thinking of those in Afghanistan. If only they could listen to us talk about them. How superficial our language is.

If I were in their situation I wouldn't bother with the solidarity offered. The ideological statements, the prayers or the silence. I would try to find the nearest escape route to survive the next days and years ahead.

Escaping with our lives. Through the gauntlet of the powerful know-it-all's. And the insurgents. A way of looking at history?

Rubenstein laid it out harshly. History as a cycle of violence and atrocity without end. You're either up or down. Better to be up.

The bankruptcy of (almost) everything.

On a lighter note, I'm relishing the gift Dan Berrigan brought me from his time on the movie, The Mission. Was quite honored – and surprised – when he gifted it to me. An indigenous stitched tapestry that hangs on my bedroom wall. A play on good and evil, I'm told.

Like Said, Berrigan was a performer. But not, as the movie attests, an actor!

AUGUST 16

In and out of my Chapel of Love. I need to keep moving this morning. Writing as I walk the shoreline home.

Low tide dark. Light arriving. A nice breeze, stronger than usual. The ocean is louder than usual, too. Tropical storm-like weather. Collateral winds only, though. The storms are in or heading toward the Gulf.

All day yesterday and today no doubt – Afghanistan. The government has absconded. With suitcases full of cash. At least as reported.

The Taliban are in the Presidential Palace. A Biblical scene. Will Moses and Aaron arrive?

What a mess it is. With the severest of consequences. Imperial power plus imperial religion. Mostly silence on our theological front. Too complicated.

Is Afghanistan liberationist theology's Bermuda Triangle?

With the Other Nations, scrap theology. Go practical. What to do now.

The romance with everything. Should be discarded. If you're caught in the middle, survival is the key. The loudest are far away. They already got out. They're Somewhere Safe.

Walking the shoreline. Writing. The birds near the water. The sound of the waves.

Thinking: The history of Surviving Calamity.

Thinking: The history of Being on the Other Side of History.

Thinking: Do not apply the indigenous Jewish prophetic to the Other Nations.

AUGUST 17

In and out of my Chapel of Love. Back issues again, though improving somewhat. Standing up from a sitting position is painful. Legs reasonably strong. Parkinson's retreat? The most important thing.

So I write as I walk the shoreline. My fellow beach walkers who notice might be curious. To know what's up.

A nice breeze cooling me. A cruise ship heading into port. Ordinary sky so far.

Afghanistan dominating the news. Airport scenes. Biden speaking from the White House. Defiant. Too simple for sure. What other kind of message can elected officials deliver?

The political details of our world. So consequential. Those who experience them. Those who watch the images. Of.

Haiti. The death toll climbs.

Everyone trying to find refuge. Solid ground.

Those whose luck holds. Luck that drops into our laps.

Those who don't make it. Who had a chance and blew it. Those who never had a chance.

God as refuge. For those on the run.

Who to trust. Since we can barely trust ourselves. If we're honest.

Trust in God. Facts on the ground too often say something different.

Will the last Afghans and Haitians, be first? I won't bet my life on it. Would you?

The perils of Strong Theology. The alternative Weak Theology. A deflection, I think.

Guardrails proffered. When they free us. When they imprison us.

Parsing the difference.

Painting my 4½" by 4½" paper sheets. My latest. I wonder if painting is a life. Or a substitute for.

Balancing the news that happens to others. With the news that happens to us.

The news we make. Now. Once upon a time. Old news that comes around. Again.

Birds gathered on the shore. Flying.

Peaceful here. Not there.

AUGUST 18

Third day in a row. In and out of my Chapel of Love. Back issues continue. Doctor's appointment tomorrow.

A loud boom box serenade greets me in my Chapel. Three cyclists getting ready for the next leg of their journey.

Up way too early – 2:45! Waiting for light. Fortunately, I fell back asleep. In my sleep journey dreams of being displaced from my campus office. No transparency. An old friend is with me, trying to figure things out.

Excited by a find in my garbage area. Twenty small blue tiles. Already started painting the first one. I'm excited by the find and the new art venture.

Birds on the shoreline as I walk. Talking to one another about their day ahead, no doubt.

Afghanistan news continues. Everyone with an opinion. On the American side, the political fallout will continue in the coming days.

The human rights of girls, women. Universal? Western? Colonial?

Romancing Islam. Christianity. Hinduism. Buddhism. Judaism. Our mistake.

Romancing modernity, secularity. Also a mistake.

"Getting Out: A History."

Discovering our freedom. Inalienable?

Young lovers, holding hands, strolling the shoreline. Better to be there or to observe?

"Romancing Love: A Journey."

Out of nowhere in particular lines from a poem I wrote in 1973 arrive: "For I have seen the lonely ones/Pacing in their rooms at dawn."

Our different seasons.

Thoughts at daybreak. The sun, for now, behind the clouds.

Walking slowly. August muggy arrived.

AUGUST 20

Strange day. No visit to my Chapel of Love. Though I did take a peek-view outside my gate this morning. Which I remember this evening as I write.

Yes, I've been grounded for a few days. My doctor's visit confirms I have a muscle strain. Where it came from I don't know but I had a similar strain three years ago. Without knowing how to manage it, I had the most painful night I have ever experienced. I'm more relaxed now and a better pain manager. Live and learn. Sometimes.

After the doctor's visit, I painted, read a bit and tried to relax. I had a John Prine-fest, especially, his song, Speed of the Sound of Loneliness.

"So what in the world's come over you?/And what in heaven's name have you done?" Simply stated. A song of understanding, wonderment. Forgiveness?

Getting stuck is human. Going rogue is human. Academic starched collars – including on the Left – they're thought inhibitors. The professionalization of education. Education as a profession. Has its limits. I don't see it surviving as is.

I recorded my own rendition of the John Prine song and sent it to a few people. No need to worry about keeping my day job!

Am I lost without my morning walk? To some extent, yes. I do like sharing the beauty I experience. As part of my late style vocation.

Is sharing the beauty I experience a downsizing of my contribution to the world around me? Depends who you ask.

The beauty of the world. With so much working against it. I've decided to stick with beauty.

Late morning. Though grounded for the long hauls, I'm still taking short walks to my beach crossover and to the ocean shore. Low tide beauty now, the sun shining bright. White light, so strong the surroundings look dark. Not yet August hot but in an hour will be. Like deep Fall north. You feel the weather before it arrives.

What to do in the still-dark morning except prepare for morning's glory? When I travel, I adjust quickly to a new routine. Being in the same place with such a change is weird. It will only be a few days, I hope. I should use these days as preparation for the no-walk Parkinson's future that will inevitably arrive.

The pandemic news continues to alarm. I pity the hospital workers, out of sight to most of us. Like prisoners and prison guards.

So much of our reality is out of sight. Though only partially now since we do see quite a bit through our virtual screens. To help make things real. Up close. Or, up close, less real. Farther away?

Like Afghanistan. US soldiers speak. Desperate to save Afgans who helped them. As if Afghanistan is right around their corner. As if war is personal – only. As if they arrived in Afghanistan on an overnight bus.

Shabbat arrives tonight. Also virtual if I Zoom into Tzedek Chicago. If Tzedek is in session tonight, which isn't always the case.

At a distance. My religiosity. Plus and minus.

How to add things up. Through subtraction.

As life falls. Away.

AUGUST 21

Shabbat. Still grounded. What to do when your local spiritual life is upended. Can certain rituals – public or private – be that important. Be the difference we need?

All of us live on the edge. Of.

Whether we are aware or not. Whatever our profession or circumstance. All of us are one step ahead – or behind – the collapse of meaning.

Which is where I am these days. One step away. From.

Feeling bereft, last night, I Zoomed into Tzedek Chicago's Friday night candle lighting. And to my surprise landed in a breakout session with a young songster who transcribes Bob Marley into Jewish. Quite a scene.

The youth of it all, I thought. Fervor. The hope for an Other way of life. Which I have, for all practical purposes, left behind. Inspiring. And Rabbi Rosen's healing prayer. I listened intently. Hoping.

Then this morning, again, in need, I Zoomed into Tzedek's Torah study. And found Deuteronomy waiting. With that rebellious child in our sights.

What to do with punishment and all sorts of other Deuteronomic goings on. Explicated – deflected? – by the rabbis, then and now.

Face it – Deuteronomy is rough going.

While listening, I painted my way through the thicket. My 4½" by 4½" paintings. Three of them. Since Deuteronomy and the Torah in general are filled with darkness and light. And we know that when we encounter either darkness or light. The other is on its way.

Since the need for and the appearances of the prophets. Who are. Darkness and light. We know the prophets will either be disappearing from the scene or will be on their way.

So a Tzedek night and day it has been. With my own *tikkun* and the world's. Darkness and light. Near and far.

AUGUST 22

Sunday, still grounded. Yesterday was miserable. Being shut in. Time dragged. Today is looking somewhat better. Painting, reading, resting.

Do I break out tomorrow?

Listening to a sermon by a former student. Lutheran minister. Bright, thoughtful and a hard worker. From the livestream, the church he's preaching in looks huge. Like the ones I first saw in Tallahassee in 1970. I couldn't figure out what the buildings were – they seemed to take up a city block. Could churches be that big? I wondered what went on in those huge church buildings?

Over time I realized the buildings formed a complex, a campus of sorts, with many parts. I thought about the money involved. Where did the money come from? Were these churches run like businesses?

Later I gave a sermon in a Black church on the other side of the tracks, so to speak. Let's just say it was considerably smaller. And poorer.

My student's sermon was about Joshua and the victors at Shechem – how easy faith is in victory! But, he asked, what of loss and faith. Natural disasters, disease, and so on. The sermon theme, quite Lutheran, is that faith is a given, via grace; faith isn't earned. Or lost. The sustaining power is God. Through Jesus Christ.

Obviously, I'm an (un)believer in this – as a Jew. Would I believe it if I were a Christian? Christianity has often seemed to me an easy way out.

Bias?

Martin Luther, the great anti-Semite, occupies a special place in my Jewish consciousness. Not a good place. Not even close.

I often wonder what clerics of all faiths believe. And don't believe. What they present to their congregations. What they share in off-the-record conversations. The easy "yes," I believe. The caveats. And, too, the disbelief. In.

I thank God for the off-the-record conversations I've had with believing Christians. Who doubt. Grateful!

What do I believe? Could I share my believing disbelief before this same congregation and survive? Maybe as a guest. One stop. But that's most of my life anyway. Among Jews, too. One stop. Run for my life!

Behind the scenes. On the run. Is that where (most) religious truth resides?

Religion as a profession. Academic and political life as well. Perhaps public performance of all sorts is a ritual hiding. Of doubt.

Liturgy as closeted performance. Always? Giving the congregation – audience? – what it expects. Needs?

Often with a tweak. A twist of sorts. Sneaking stuff in. That changes the trajectory. For those who notice.

Today, for example, my former student noted that Shechem is the modern-day Palestinian city, Nablus. Since he lived and worked in Palestine for years, perhaps a coded message that Palestinians are real.

Good to see my former students hitting the Gospel trail in various denominational traditions. Do I travel with them?

Respect, from a distance. Stuck inside, I observe.

The truth is supposed to set us free. If we could discern "the" truth. Does it?

AUGUST 23

3:08 AM. Up. After tossing and turning for too long. The world – my world – here and there. But not everywhere.

I think I'll keep a running log today. To see my grounding through. I did make it to the crossover yesterday. I will venture out again today.

For me, sanity is through the written word. Painting the world as I see it. Listening to the news. Trying to shut it out as well. Remembering everything. Like John Prine.

I wonder if remembrance is a way of leaving what should be left behind. Or simply a way of transforming pain into a deeper reckoning.

Continuing to read Leonard Bernstein's letters. It's 1965, the year of his Chichester Psalms. Many letters back and forth with the Dean of the Cathedral there. Early interfaith. The choir to sing in Hebrew. Would that offend? Bernstein queries.

I was welcomed at the same Cathedral decades later and spoke to a full house. On a Jewish theology of liberation. A sign of the times. Progress or decline?

After all, Bernstein headed up the Israel Philharmonic in its early years. I wonder what Bernstein would think if he heard me speak. Would I be music to his ears? What kind?

What Israel has become. What Israel was. The distance traveled. As it evolved. As it was from the beginning?

What Bernstein knew and when he knew it.

Also reading Martha Gellhorn and her reporting from Dachau as the war ended. Still quite fresh. Disturbing to put it mildly. Her wandering through Germany after the war; her take on the Nuremberg trials. Yesterday I ordered a collection of her letters. Strong writer.

Thinking of my travels through Germany decades later on a Jewish theology of liberation. A different landscape to be sure. Germany, though, still haunted. Forever?

Traveling Jewish. Then and now. Always a risk. Always an opportunity.

What to do with the sea change in Jewish life. The corner Jewish turned. What seemed to be a new beginning. Empowerment. Becoming the end. Of.

Can ethical Jewish history be reborn? If so, what could this possibly mean. For Jews. For the world.

A Jewish return to an ethical path is to be desired. Can it be if Jewish carries with it the burdens of occupation and ethnic cleansing? Christians, some, think they can or have been reborn ethically. After their much longer decline. If so, what does this rebirth mean?

I wonder if patterns of decline and rebirth, shared across the lines, the lines once drawn, now, for all practical purposes obsolete – are they worth the time spent speculating upon? Better perhaps to let things go down. See what we find at the bottom.

Since we're all at the bottom, I suppose.

Late afternoon. Still grounded. Almost ready to play? I hesitate.

At noon I took a drive and ended up at the nearby riverside park. I walked for a few minutes, enjoying the scenery, as much as one can in the August heat. Then drove back home.

Reading the obituaries I see that Don Everly of the Everly Brothers is no more. The brothers were innovators on the music scene, though they seem quite tame by those who followed. Yet enduring. A beautiful-voiced duo. RIP.

In the Bernstein letters, it's March 1966. Bernstein is in Vienna conducting Falstaff at the Vienna State Opera. He's enjoying himself, as he did most everywhere he went, and is being received as a charismatic, almost heroic figure, again, as was often the case.

But in Vienna, Bernstein is conflicted by his celebrity. Writing to his father and mother, Bernstein is "enjoying Vienna enormously – as much as a Jew can. There are so many memories here; one deals with so many ex-Nazis (and maybe still Nazis); and you never know if the public that is screaming bravo for you might contain someone who 25 years ago might have shot me dead. But it's better to forgive, and if possible, forget. The city is so beautiful and full of tradition. Everyone here lives for music, especially opera, and I seem to be the new hero. What they call the 'Bernstein Wave' that has swept Vienna has produced some strange results; all of a sudden it's fashionable to be Jewish."

I notice the year, 1966, as I always do. The year Rubenstein's *After Auschwitz* was published. As I now think, after participating in a truncated Zoom remembrance of Rubenstein who died recently, the birth pangs of my Jewish theology of liberation are found there.

Strange, my first extended travel to Germany, by invitation of Dorothee Soelle, was 1986, twenty years after Bernstein's conflicted triumph. I arrived within weeks of the Chernobyl disaster and was midway through writing my Jewish theology of liberation.

So time changes much, if less than everything. Jewish Bernstein being celebrated in the land of the Holocaust. Could ex-Nazis really love Jews? I was also welcomed as a Jew, though not as a hero. I grappled with another sea change in Jewish history in nearly the very same place.

There were Germans who welcomed me in Germany and later in Austria, too. Could I trust their welcome?

How to find the words for this sea change. Without simply flipping off the recent past. Germany was – still – weird for Jews. Certainly for me. Marked by Holocaust theology – still – I don't fit – still – with those who, too easily, leave history out of the state of Israel equation.

My, my, I didn't think my Day 5 Grounding would turn into a meditation on Germany/Austria, Bernstein, *After Auschwitz* and a Jewish theology of liberation. Retro City?

I go my own way. With, admittedly, diminishing results. But who among the oppressed, including Palestinians, embraces wholeheartedly, Jews who cease to speak historically. Or sweep Jewish history aside in a universalist thrust. As if Jewish history collapses completely into every category other than its own?

AUGUST 24

Waking. Almost 5, I lay out my breakfast vegetables and bread as if preparing for my sunrise walk. I'm not ready, though. My back issues are on the mend, perhaps even ready for my routine. I'm holding back a bit, making sure.

I awoke with a feeling of loss. And gratitude. A strange combination difficult to explain. Like so much in life, connections aren't obvious. Perhaps that's the way we hold things together. Apart.

"What in the world's come over you." John Prine, country wordsmith, still resonating. We can't really deal with this quite human question. Something came over me – a while ago. To my grave it will go. Defining.

When I first spoke out many years ago – what came over me then? I didn't map things out, if maps there were. Friends were worried as to what may come over me from outside. I was puzzled. Why worry? What came over me was inside.

Initially, I didn't get their worry equation. Later, it was a combination, inner and from outside.

How to explain the mysteries of our lives. Commitments and trauma. Brokenness. Loss and, sometimes, gratitude.

In the middle of last night, I was up painting "My Starry Night." Two or three of them. Blasphemy? Not copies, just my Vincent.

Also writing my journal. With paint.

Awaiting light. All our lives. In one way or another.

Late afternoon. August hot. Being grounded in August is double-duty boring. I might venture out for a short walk a bit later. Tomorrow morning I'm aiming for a full return, if I can make it to my Chapel of Love, on Shabbat which is my birthday – 69 years old, I'll be. Better late than never.

News of the day. Pandemic. Pfizer is now approved. Vaccinations to follow. It can't be soon enough. Afghanistan – trauma continues. Should the entire country be evacuated? Progressive cable news seems to think so.

Speaking of soon, Tzedek announced its Yom Kippur line-up today. The program includes a Palestinian of note and an up and coming African American thinker in dialogue. I assume their discussion will focus on the Palestinian situation and the alliances necessary to move things forward.

For decades I argued in speech and text that synagogues should do these things – especially on Yom Kippur, our Confession/Judgment Day. Tzedek has stepped up to the plate. A strong witness. Important.

Yet, when the news flashed across my screen, my depression about being grounded deepened. It wasn't about the effort or the speakers themselves. Rather it was the sense I've had for a decade and more, and increasingly, that it's all too late. Very much so. And that somehow continuing on like this simply reinforces the too-lateness.

Israel's occupation of Palestine. Is permanent.

Of course, the situation is ongoing. It needs to be addressed. And others could say about my own dissent years ago. That it was already too late then. Which may be true. Probably is.

How does our dissent function? I rarely see this question raised. Will those who speak now name the elephant in the room – that the occupation is permanent? Perhaps they will start there and ask: What can be done within this permanent occupation?

I'm all ears this Yom Kippur. If I tune in. Yom Kippur is so depressing anyway. Should I risk a further devolution of spirit?

Anyway, it's been a long time since anyone invited me to speak on Yom Kippur. For good reason!

It was 1991, at Union Theological Seminary. Long story it is. Only to say, with the Jewish Theological Seminary across the block, I've never been invited back.

Perhaps best I go quiet. Into Yom Kippur's dark night.

Coming to the end of Bernstein's letters. It's 1971 and the telephone, including long-distance, has become low-cost and easy. Letters are fewer and farther between. Bernstein dies in 1990 but the last decades of his letters only cover 50 pages or so. His end isn't pretty.

So it goes.

AUGUST 25

Moonlight. My first, first light, in a week.

Left home this morning just before 6 for a short walk. Less than 30 minutes. Part of my return. I felt good, though my walking legs need to regain their strength and stability. I was swaying out there. Like I was a bit tipsy. But so glad to feel the early morning breeze, the smell and sound of the ocean. Moonlight lighting the darkness.

What I miss is telling me something important about my life. Moving parts of the physical and spiritual. Without piety or creed. No rescue. Life, though. More life.

Now home. Thinking about the day ahead. Reading Gellhorn last night. She's in China, with Japan knocking on China's door. Then Italy, with Germans also knocking. No special pleading from Gellhorn. A war reporter she is; her travels aren't for the faint of heart.

What Gellhorn sees and reports on. What she survives.

Harrowing, the destruction of war. Always.

AUGUST 26

Is first light enough?

This morning I was out and about a little longer than yesterday. On the backroads, then home on the beach. Dark and rainy. Ocean loud. Wind strong. Has a storm blown into my Cape paradise?

Back twinges. Something is loose there. Doable. Though I'm not sure if tomorrow's birthday boy will make it to his Chapel of Love. We shall see.

Thinking as I walked: "Can a person lose faith without becoming cynical?"

Cynicism is the conspiracy dead-end road I've never entered. I won't. Since there's no future there. For me or my children – the world.

And no bridge. Out of there either.

In many ways I've lost faith. In. Though I don't feel cynical. About. I hold both together. Itself, a faith in?

This morning. First light is enough.

AUGUST 27

Shabbat Shalom!

69 years old!

This morning, rain. I'm heading to a family friend's home for the weekend. Where we'll go through an archive treasure trove of my (very) early writing, letters home and photographs he recently discovered. To be reported on later.

Gratitude for the Facebook birthday greetings. Many sides of that virtual coin.

Quite a birthday. Waking to meet the sunrise but raining, so off earlier than expected. I'm hitting the highway for the first time in almost 2 years. Looking around at the world. The (un)beach dark sky.

At home, we eat some Colombian sweets and bread. Then look through what he recently found through family digging. Papers, letters and photos of mine, I haven't seen in years.

And lo and behold, what turns up? My box of pastels from childhood. Still in the box I remember from 60 years ago. Also, one of my father's late paintings. When things were becoming more difficult. He, too, a Parkinson's sufferer.

Birthday presents. Including a sturdy Zen meditation bench. A lovely birthday call from my younger son.

And yes, I did carry through on my birthday commitment – giving gifts to others on my birthday. My gift for my eldest was one of my back-of-the-envelope paintings. He chose it because it featured my favorite color – blue.

I have one more gift to send. To a former student, from way back when. She just published her first book. Interesting backstory. An evangelical upbringing. Quite white with a Chinese father. Her struggle to redefine her "whiteness." Her escape route. Where to land is another story.

I didn't listen to one note of news today.

So many nice birthday greetings. Pizza dinner. Long chats about life. More to come tomorrow.

How far I've come. To find at times. The simple things in life that matter.

AUGUST 28

Shabbat. Waking. In the spare bedroom. Officially on my way to 70.

The scenery is quite different here. Oak trees rather than palm trees. No ocean sounds. A manmade lake outside. At night bats fly rather than morning seagulls. Pretty in its own, different, way.

My friend is off to rehearsal. He's producing an upcoming theatrical event. I am alone in a different space. About to go back through the memories brought to me yesterday. Some fun, others not. My running commentary was taped on each item as they were presented. More stuff to go through later today.

It seems that the direction memory goes is dependent on present circumstances. So summing up, as I – we – periodically do, is contextual. Even after we've gone. Away.

How far do we go when we go away?

I placed my father's late Parkison's-tinged painting at my bedside last night. The binoculars he brought home from his service in World War II are in the living room nearby.

Parts of my past are close at hand. And part of me, also nearby, is past as well. Past meets past – an interesting encounter.

My father was an aircraft gunner in World War II. I used to joke about his terrible eyesight and his ability to see and aim at oncoming aircraft. I had fun teasing him. But for my father the war wasn't about laughs. He traveled by ship to Europe – no doubt in a tight fit with thousands of servicemen – and slept in tents in the cold British and French countryside, as he recalled. At the end of the war, he was stationed in Germany, mostly guarding German prisoners. My father had no time for the Germans, to put it mildly – and never romanticized the army. My father wasn't a macho man. I think now, in a way I hadn't thought before, that he was deeply scarred by the war.

The pastels I grew up, like his binoculars, are parts of my childhood. When I began my painter's journey, I started with pastels I remembered from childhood. Full circle?

Among other items found is a poem I wrote at the Catholic Worker – or at least it was typed there. It must have been just after my arrival in New York and is typed on Catholic Worker stationary. The poem is addressed to Sonia of Dostoevsky's *Crime and Punishment* and is about my loneliness and search – still near at hand. Quite romantic. I was young.

We taped my reading of the poem. And it's dated, quite coincidentally, I'm sure, on my birthday that year – 8/27/1974.

Much to process.

Or let go.

AUGUST 29

Up just after 6. First light delayed.

Yesterday more memories. To be brought to other members of the family. Stretching back 50 years plus. Is what was, still?

In the late afternoon we took a swim in the pool. Good to relax. Good for my still troublesome back. A long discussion poolside. Saying things that had been said already. Around the edges. A confessional in some ways.

High wire, though. Without a religious net.

Do I have a legacy to project, protect? What is the future of one's afterlife in our virtual world. Where there is more. And more. And more. Still more. A daily avalanche. Of.

Reading through my newly re-found college Senior Thesis yesterday, I realize again how far advanced my children are at the same age in their journey. Far surpassing me. As it should be.

Today I'm going home. After an IKEA visit to scope out a new sleeper couch. I've only been to an IKEA store once before and experienced it as a labyrinth without a center. You have to focus. Lest you be overcome. By yet another avalanche. Of.

Did I forget our evening ice cream splurge – soft-serve vanilla dipped in chocolate? Hadn't had one in years. So filling I skipped dinner.

I started my take on my father's late painting. Using the pastels rescued from my childhood. I will be adding my new pastels, watercolor and acrylic during the week. An homage to my (un)famous father.

Or should I leave my unfinished initial effort as it is? Walking by my drawing several times yesterday and now this morning, I begin to like it unfinished. As memory is.

A great 69th. About to return to my real world.

AUGUST 30

Home. First light. My return to the backroads, halfway to my Chapel of Love and then home on the beach. Low tide. Humid. With a morning breeze I needed. Loved the sound of the ocean as I walked.

A new Chapel of Love visitation date, Rosh Hashanah – September 6th. Unless I find earlier daylight on my beach field of struggle. Like a halfback handed the football. Only God knows when I'll break through the line.

What a birthday celebration it was! Maybe the best and most extensive of my life. Ending at my home swimming in the pool. Afterward, my friend took a solo dip in the ocean. I had to rescue him, though, after he foolhardy walked the three blocks home without flip-flops. Blister City. Lesson learned I hope.

IKEA hunting yesterday for a new sleeper couch was unsuccessful. A Sunday church-time exploration. The throngs did arrive. Modern worship. IKEA's choir!

What a store, though. Everything is a bargain. Enticing. Seductive. What a deal! I've been in the store twice now. After ten minutes or so I'm exhausted. Can we leave now?

Discussions about framing some of my art are ongoing. Also contemplating a venture to a real art store to see what professional painters use. Am I ready to graduate?

Discussions about my weight. Holding steady in the low 140s. My boys want me to gain weight but I'm eating the same and the sudden weight loss of last year seems permanent. My doctors are monitoring. Mystery, though. I dropped 25 pounds or more. The weight loss is significant.

On the national scene, Hurricane Ida is hitting Louisiana big time. My God, these hurricane wallops are devastating. I hope the rebuilt levees hold our altered nature's siege.

On the international scene, the bodies of the US military men killed in Afghanistan are home now. The US withdrawal is only days away. I can't imagine the death of a son. I've always been against a volunteer army. If war it is, everyone has to be on the line. To make sure war is worth it.

Does anybody really think about the relation of God and nature anymore? Of God and war?

I recently read that the saintly Jonathan Edwards owned slaves. Another revelation.

Time-bound we all are, aren't we? Especially when we think we're fancy free.

Found in the family archive trove, the plastic toy Torah on top of my bar mitzvah reception cake. Fifty-six years after the fact.

Torah icing.

When this miniature plastic Torah was found, and I was asked if I could place it, my mind went blank. Where could it have come from? Then a hunch. So I checked my bar mitzvah photo album and there it was, right in front of me. We found the bar mitzvah reception menu, too. In mint condition. As if it was yesterday.

There are many stories surrounding my bar mitzvah and the reception at the then world famous Eden Roc Hotel in Miami Beach, which we couldn't afford. The Eden Roc represented my mother's aspiration of the upward mobility we never achieved. Perhaps this extravagant reception was to impress my mother's sister, who was elegant and wealthy. Though my uncle and aunt on my father's side were also in attendance. Card-carrying members of the Communist Party they were. As well, my grandmother and grandfather, who, with their parents, as children, arrived in America fleeing the Pale of Settlement or thereabouts.

I often think my Jewish theology of liberation was born in the shadow of Richard Rubenstein's teaching on the Holocaust. Now I think it had earlier stirrings, in Hebrew school, leading to my bar mitzvah.

My Hebrew school teachers didn't have much of a clue. Nor did the parents of my generation. That the Halakhah of Unintended Consequences was in play.

That law when applied to Jewish youth? In a nutshell: When you place Jewish kids in the path of assimilationist upper mobility, many will answer the call with a liberal sensibility. But there will always be those who embrace the indigenous Jewish prophetic, turned inward, as a critique of Jewish life. Without, at first, knowing why. And, mostly, without a second thought.

For the indigenous Jewish prophetic is always right there waiting to be embraced. And embodied.

In our time, what other reason is there to be Jewish than to draw near, to embrace and to embody the prophetic?

And get this: At the end of ethical Jewish history the children of those who embody the Jewish prophetic may even be "worse."

As I know well.

AUGUST 31

Home now. And yes, I made it back to my Chapel of Love this morning. After more than a week on standby. But I didn't tarry there – I only took time for my prayer. I didn't write on my walk home either. I had to keep focused. Step by step.

Pretty it was, first light. With birds on the low tide shore. The sky opened wide as I entered the Chapel. The sun rose on my walk home. Good weather. A nice breeze. Fairly low humidity. For the last day of August.

Hurricane season intensifies in September. Ida has already arrived on the Gulf Coast with tremendous winds and rain. New Orleans seems to have survived. Power outages are being reported in so many homes. Other troubles too. I know what this means, having experienced hurricanes and their aftermath. Waiting for light, I have been at times – with a different meaning than dawn.

The US is out of Afghanistan, more or less. Refugees galore. Were Afghans who worked with the US, dupes. Of American imperialism – only?

I'm very low on the continuum of American interventionism. In fact, I won the Florida State championship debate title in 1970 on that very topic – whether US interventionism was ever justified. Though admittedly, I can't remember whether I argued affirmative or negative in the title clincher.

I've been thinking about Said's understanding of Orientalism and how that term is bandied about now. With reference to Afghanistan and the internal struggles there. Including those who left on US planes and the many more who want out. Ultimate hoped-for destination is the US or Europe. So Afghanistan might be an interesting test case for complicating just what Orientalism is. Has become. Or was.

A test case for Islam too? And what is said and can/not be said about the complexity of Islam in the interfaith circles that abound. Since, in these circles, mostly we romanticize all religions involved, why not romanticize Islam? The World Parliament of Religions scenario.

So many interfaith ecumenical deals to be made. We're drowning in them.

On another note, my volume of Martha Gellhorn's letters has arrived. I started reading last night, and her letters are everything I thought they would be – long and strong. The letters start in 1930 – Gellhorn is in her twenties – and she's already traveling and in love – with a married man. Trying to figure out her future as a woman and as a writer.

On April 29, 1934, she writes to a friend what I think is a good definition of a writer in general: "I am writing you to see for myself; I am writing to myself through you."

Indeed, the writing life. Perhaps the walking life, too. The painting life?

SEPTEMBER 1

My friend's birthday light. Just a few days after mine. Pastel sky, pretty.

Are there certain first light skies that match our personalities?

I didn't make it to my Chapel of Love. A creeping high tide was part of it. Light back issues. I felt Parkinson's sluggish. Lazy?

Tides change. Time change. The sun is rising later, a bit after 7. I still rise at 4, give or take. Too much wait time. Daylight Savings Time is right around the bend, though. Salvation?

Thinking as I walked of those early years with my two boys. They define and challenge me. My fondest memories.

Before them, I had no idea about children. Now I don't know what it would be like to exist without them.

When I leave this life, I'll leave them behind. A strange feeling.

If I believed in resurrection, at least I'd be able to check in on them now and again. A death-bed conversion it would have to be.

Can resurrected Christians be in contact with their still living children?

Committed thinkers my children are. A given, I always thought. Was there an alternative?

My pride and joy, though, is that both were excellent baseball players. Like I was, if memory serves!

Gellhorn's letters. Still in the 1930s. Gellhorn has struck up a friendship with Eleanor Roosevelt, who is now receiving quite a few – very long – letters from her. It's December 1936 and Gellhorn is vacationing in Key West with her recently widowed mother. As fate would have it, Gellhorn runs into Ernest Hemingway in a bar. Soon she'll be traveling with him to Spain. I anticipate fireworks wherever she goes.

Yesterday Biden's speech on the end of the war in Afghanistan. Strong, defiant. Congress is digging deep into the January 6th goings on. Will it investigate its very own? The Texas abortion law is now on the books.

Today I had a long counseling session on a vocation to the priesthood with a former student. So complex it is, charting our individual lives. Especially when God and much else are involved. Meaningful discussion. With all the faults of the Catholic Church, such vocations are important to discern.

So much going on in the world. For others to deal with. I'm watching the world go round and round. Commenting on it, too.

Thinking that though I was never much of a letter writer, like the letters I love to read, my journals, faithfully kept over the years, may be the "letters" I send to myself.

Dipping into Samuel Beckett. Meditating on his line: "It is winter. Without journey."

But for me, through thick and thin, the journey hasn't ended.

What is life when the journey ends?

SEPTEMBER 2

In my Chapel of Love. With heavy rains last night, the sea air refreshes me. Tide is doable this morning. Pretty blue sky. Light arriving. Grateful for life.

Prayer said. Careful on the steps. Coming and going. I can't afford another fall.

Painting yesterday. An early Jackson Pollack, A Cup of Tea (1946), appeared on my screen. I had a go at it. Lots of color. His before. My after.

Other paintings last night, just letting my brush wander here and there.

Absorbed in Gellhorn's letters. The war is heating up and, in her travels, she's with and without Hemingway. Reading her articles for Collier's. She's among the Dutch now, again painting a vivid picture of war: its brutality, stupidity, cowardice and courage.

Gellhorn is writing more letters to Eleanor Roosevelt. Admiring her but not pulling any punches. Did Gellhorn's palling around with Roosevelt trigger my dream last night where I had an extended conversation with Barack Obama?

An NPR segment on the Brazilian President, Mussolini wannabe, Bolsonaro and his biker rallies. Quite a hoot. If it wasn't so serious. Brazil seems to be an updated Wild, Wild West.

Rosh Hashanah right around the weekend corner. Then Yom Kippur. Trying to keep it light this year. Hoping that my Little Engine That Could. Will.

Since there won't be any real communal confession. And any real confession made – by those few brave souls. Is tainted and too late.

What we and others have won't be given up. Rituals aside, our confessions, even if well intentioned, help enable our continued entanglement. So I have come to believe. Where else is there to go?

When I look at the world and dissent, perspective is essential. The means of production, power and the demands of ordinary life, will mostly win. Even as our losses mount.

The prophetic is not about overcoming loss. The prophet carries loss within – and keeps on.

When railing against everything becomes perpetual, our compromised landscape becomes obvious and exposed.

Right now, though, a deep blue sky. A wonderful breeze. The sounds of ocean life.

A take on Albert Camus's rendering of Sisyphus: Imagine Marc happy.

Evening now. Reading. It's September 6, 1940. Gellhorn writes to a former lover about her life with Ernest Hemingway. Commenting about his soon to be published book, *For Whom the Bell Tolls*, Gellhorn writes: "E's book has been an agony, like having children without interruption for months and months. I am tired in my head with it. I don't think anyone can be a great writer and do great books without pulling down the pillars of the temple all over the place."

SEPTEMBER 3

Up late. It's 6 already!!! After a night of tumultuous dreams, one frightening, the other sad. Without endings. As dreams go.

Without endings. Another way of ending?

Now in my Chapel of Love. The sun is rising as I write. Simple sky. Plain. Shabbat up ahead.

Yesterday I listened to a Days of Awe preview. Conversations to ready us for the Big Days ahead. About home and homelessness in the Jewish tradition.

Diaspora narrative. Beware of the state!

Contemplating Deuteronomy's ending and the ample warnings that abound. What to do with home. What to do without home.

Moses on his last legs. Joshua at the ready. The prophets in the shadows. It won't be long before they start appearing.

Our ancient texts. Filled with everything. Dangerous. Very soon these texts won't be ours alone. Another danger.

If only our texts had remained in-house.

The Torah narrative is too explosive. I doubt it could have remained where it was.

Christianity. A break-away. Inevitable?

Christianity. Jewish (un)housed. Roaming. Too far, too wide. Danger multiplied.

Christianity's claim to universality as its least admirable and most dangerous trait.

Yahweh. A Mountain God. More or less. Traveling.

Yahweh as a Traveling Mountain God.

Tribes. Tribal Confederacy. Samuel.

Images: Burning bush. Moses and Aaron in the palace. Elijah's ravens.

Ezekiel's scroll. Of doom. That tastes just like honey.

Jesus a renegade Jew. At least as portrayed. That Jesus came to save the Gentiles is a late addition.

Lots more to think through. More than enough.

Walking home now. The sun is rising hot. My back's acting up a bit. Legs okay. We shall see about tomorrow's journey.

For now. Trying to regain my footing. Within.

SEPTEMBER 4

Shabbat. Waking, 5:30, up and around, but in for the day. No Chapel of Love. No backroads walk. Back issues yesterday which became worse as I walked. Took a pill when I returned and things quieted down. It wasn't awful as it had been. I took it as a warning. I need to be patient.

Yesterday I hit a wall. I was stuck without a future. Alone, with my books and paintings. Summer days are too long.

I'm safe, though, which is a big thing. Listening to news reports about Ida in Louisiana, New York and New Jersey. Terrible flooding, without power for days and more, water rescues. Those who weren't rescued.

Hurricanes and their onslaught. Aftermath. The rest of September and October is hurricane season still. Last year my Cape avoided it all. I pray for that missing again.

Not to forget the corruption attending the after-hurricane cleanups. The companies that come in overcharge the insurance companies and individual contractors do as well. The honest ones are few and far between. In condos. money often exchanges hands between the contractors and those who make the decisions. Management companies are involved. A racket.

What would we do without corruption? This is the other side of the coin. Sometimes I think corruption makes the world go round. Best to negotiate corruption.

I'm using my son's gifted baseball glove, which was his when he was an up and coming baseball player. I roam my apartment with glove on hand, pounding the baseball and throwing it up in the air. I'm catching it fine. The test will be outside when he gets a new glove for himself.

Hand-eye coordination. I'm nervous about it. Since there came a time when both of my boys began throwing so hard I had to slow them down. I'm at another age completely now. Soft toss is the limit now.

Sitting Zen this morning. I've been sitting the last few nights but let it go last night. Two ways – on a cushion and on the bench gifted me.

My birthday gifts are changing. On a previous visit, my younger son brought me some beautiful wind chimes. Positioned right with the AC and fans, they enliven my place with wonderful sounds.

Watching first light arrive. Sitting. A way of negotiating the drama of the High Holidays. What better way to greet the Days of Awe than silence?

Will be reading more Gellhorn today. Chatty letters but always about real stuff. Yesterday I read some of her letters to Hemingway and friends where she mused about the limits of intimacy in general and marriage in particular. Her take on intimacy and marriage? While granting some kind of security, marriage itself is problematic.

For Gellhorn, intimacy tends to close down conversation and honesty rather than, as advertised, increase it. Where anything could be thought or said when untethered, limits are now in place.

Another example I suppose of the Law of Unintended Consequences. Like the solemn days that lead to Yom Kippur where we witness the confession that isn't really a confession. Or is not what it should be. Or is way too late. As the shofar sounds.

Afternoon. It's September 22, 1941. Gellhorn writes from Cuba to a friend about her would-be memoirs: "I started to write memoirs, addressing them to you, since I can always talk to you. But the memoirs cooled off, because I knew what I was doing, and if there are any rests left, on paper, of my life, they will have to be like this, disjointed and uncertain, done for no reason, and put in an envelope to mail. I cannot do the other."

Gellhorn continues: "When I start to think, I freeze. And when I freeze I think like a lady who came from a clean, honorable, intelligent and quiet home. And what sort of writing is that?"

After sitting Zen, breakfast and painting, and with a reminder tip from a friend who is thinking about converting to Judaism – converts of all types are so observant! So I tuned into Tzedek's Torah study, the last of the Jewish year. And found Rabbi Rosen expounding on Deuteronomy 30, the supreme warning passage of the many warning passages in the Torah.

So many warnings, I thought, as the chapter was read aloud. As if our Israel sky is already falling or about to.

Today isn't any different. Have I, with some other Jews gone, in our own way, Deuteronomic?

My sense that we are at the end of ethical Jewish history might qualify here. I certainly feel this as intensely as Moses did. Yet Moses leaves a way forward; I don't see this for us. A close reading of Deuteronomy, especially as the Promised Land comes into view, is hardly optimistic. The deck seems stacked against Israel.

The demands in these passages, choose this way and live, choose that way and die, are dualistic in the strongest terms. They're scorched earth. What to do with this kind of God – a consistent theme of the Torah study sessions I've tuned into. As Rabbi Rosen points out – also consistently – he is and we must pick and choose what in the Torah we accept or tolerate. And what we have to reject out of hand.

Deuteronomy 30 is a classic case. But then every tradition has to do the same thing with their canonical texts and/or the history which flows from them. Picking and choosing is the lifeblood of religions and religiosity.

Years ago I wrote a book about the covenant, no doubt a strange one. Or rather my interpretation of the covenant with Palestine and Palestinians in mind. Like most of my writing it was passed over in relative silence. The Jewish world at large picks and chooses too. They don't choose Palestinians.

What to do with Deuteronomy 30 and the covenant with reference to Palestinians?

Perhaps we should broadcast our own choice under the leading headline I discovered in one of Bibles I found on my beach crossover: “Here Is What Will Happen.”

Perhaps what will happen has already.

SEPTEMBER 5

Waking again later than usual. Earlier wakings through the night. Unremembered dreams. Feeling a sadness I can't locate. Adding up to a restless night.

The aloneness of life I suppose. Even when accompanied by others. From afar.

Our virtual lives. They arrive and depart. In waves.

Speaking of virtual, yet another day off my beach trail. I did make it around the block in the afternoon yesterday. I'll try to do the same today.

My Zen time is increasing, cross-legged and on my bench. It isn't the same though as my sunrise walk. Not even close. Tomorrow I hope to try my beach walk, even halfway, and, if necessary, I'll take one of my pills afterward. Maybe I need another trip to the doctor but I doubt it's something they can do much about. Hopefully, one day, all will be righted.

Yesterday I learned that my Festschrift has arrived in the Philippines. In e-book format. Yes, I was consulted about whether to order the hardback or the e-book. I surprised myself by suggesting the latter, even though I am a devotee of books I hold in my hands.

A confession: I have never read an e-book. But thinking of use in classes and being available to other universities in the Philippines, it seems obvious. I crossed over.

I have travelled to the Philippines several times on speaking tours and teaching assignments at universities and seminaries there. Quite interesting to put it mildly. Lots of political corruption, social justice movements, piety and sophisticated religious thought. I'm fascinated by the devotion to the Black Nazarene. Much to ponder including the Philippines geopolitical situation. Not much theological thought in the US on the rise of China. In the Philippines, China can't be ignored.

News this morning of Ida and her aftermath, in the South and the North. Climate is changing. Is it obvious now to the deniers? And more importantly, what to do and quickly. A full start needed. Bold.

Pandemic news. 1500 people dying a day in the US. Booster shots on the horizon. I'm glad my children are grown. Sending kids to schools, childcare, etc. Anxiety on steroids. News of another variant discovered in Colombia.

Before sleep I read more of Gellhorn's wartime essays. It's 1944 and she is with a US fighter squadron flying missions over Germany. She flies on a mission in the dead of night, with an oxygen tank provided. Chasing enemy fighters and being chased. Flying high and wide. Diving for targets. No net.

Gellhorn's descriptions are ripe and scary. The barebones of war. Who will fly and return. Who will fly and perish. Those who carry on. War as existential dread. Existential courage.

The overall numbness of those who live through war. Witnessing too much loss.

In the throes of her Hemingway divorce, Gellhorn writes about life's disappointments and how one needs to keep moving. Gellhorn is a mover and shaker without pretensions. She needs her space. She wants to leave space for others. Her deep suspicions about intimacy abound. Especially when she wants it. Worse when someone else wants it. Mutuality isn't her thing. That's when the danger heightens.

In the summer of 1943, in a letter to Hemingway, Gellhorn refers to the desire and danger of intimacy – again when folded into marriage – as an "odd performance" – with benefits, limits and liabilities. Two years later, in the midst of divorce, she is wooing and warning another lover that what both of them want won't work. And it's precisely what they want – a life together – that's the problem. What propels these lovers is their impediment.

Gellhorn's letters are beautiful and telling. Deep and committed. And free. Few illusions. Too few? How do we live without illusions. Of some shared future?

If no shared future, cancel marriage – institutionalized or not. Cancel religion as well. The struggle for community over empire. Or community within empire. Cancelled?

In the middle of the night, I was still thinking Deuteronomy as if this and other Torah texts are relevant. Why dwell in such an ancient and convoluted textual quagmire? Certainly not for the specifics – what to do with rebellious children or how to punish those who consort with other Gods.

Deuteronomy is way too harsh and judgmental for my taste. Anyone's taste I assume. Yet the core of it all, the covenant, still resonates. If Deuteronomy isn't compelling, Jewish is.

Whatever our take, is there Jewish without Deuteronomy?

Yesterday I registered – and paid – for Tzedek's High Holiday services. I'm a bit embarrassed by my small contribution. Let's say it's a holdover from Hebrew school and the idea of paying for services. Since every synagogue is on its own financially, there may be no other way. Still, there's something wrong about paying for religion.

So High Holidays Zoom it is. Tzedek services are pretty good, a compliment coming from one is who is incredibly low on religious rituals. Especially on the Jewish front, where I believe the less the better. Zoom is very good for me. Almost perfect. Tuning in at a distance.

So, returning to the theme of the last hours, the core of life. Does our answer depend on the time of day or night?

Yesterday I painted a scene of crossing over a divide and the danger of stark beauty. Looking at the painting in the morning, I wonder what I see. In the middle of the night it made sense.

Not yet noon! I just returned from a crossover walk. It's hot but so far so good.

Walking is my lifeblood. Anxious about losing the simplest part of my life.

Walking, I thought about my Gellhorn week. I didn't even have her on my radar – hadn't heard of her – until reading a collection of the Bernstein letters. When her letter appeared, I thought, wow, she doesn't pull any punches and what strength. I heard Gellhorn's voice as an open door. To.

So I ordered the collection of her letters and I was right. Her open door extends far and wide. Now I'm looking into her biography and gathering fragments before I plunge into her life written by another.

I gather so far and to my delight that Gellhorn had Jewish background on both sides of her immediate family tree. Though so far in the letters she doesn't mention her Jewishness. Maybe that will come later. Her visit to Dachau she wrote about as the war came to an end devastated her. Later her support for Israel, as I gather so far, was unwavering. In what I've read of her essays she doesn't identify herself there as Jewish either.

Gellhorn's relations with men were varied and plentiful. Lots of affairs, though she insists that sex wasn't her cup of tea. She was attracted to the life men could and did lead. As she put it: "I daresay I was the worst bed partner in five continents."

Gellhorn had a biting sense of humor about others. And herself.

From her early letters right through, Gellhorn is explicit about her sense of intimacy – mostly expressed on the page. As is often the case with writers, she ordered her life through her writing.

In her declining years, cataracts, eventual semi-blindness and ovarian cancer brought her down. She committed suicide by swallowing cyanide. It was 1989. She was 65 years old.

More ahead in her biography I'm going to order soon. Her letters are my High Holidays reading it seems. Unexpected. A rigorous life. A chosen death.

All sorts of things can and have been read into Gellhorn's life. I try to see her and others – and myself – within a historical frame. Those who gloss over history with ahistorical declarations aren't doing anyone favors.

I painted a portrait of Gellhorn – or sketched one. Pastel soft. Too much so? Anyway, it's my Gellhorn-take for now. As her life unfolds before me. RIP.

SEPTEMBER 6

Out on the backroads this morning, I saw first light. Thank God! I did keep it simple and short. With a short excursion onto the beach. I still feel things a bit askew in my back; I need to work my way through it.

Yes, the breeze and the darkness, with light arriving – for me a sign of life, a new day ahead. If that light goes out, I'll find myself in another darkness to navigate.

Passages of life. Corners to turn.

So, reviving, if tentative. I'll see how my day goes. Going slow has advantages I suppose. Savoring the less. As more.

Rosh Hashanah arrives tonight. Shana Tova! What will the New Year bring? More of the same I suppose. Do we ever have a fresh start?

My Zoom link to Tzedek's services hasn't arrived yet. Though services begin tomorrow. I used to look for excuses to miss services. Still do when they're in person. I wonder though what I'll do if the algorithm doesn't find me.

Labor Day. People were already arriving for their beach day out as I headed home.

September 11th coming into view – 20th anniversary this year. So much death then. And after. With Afghanistan in recent view – soon to be forgotten – how we forgot Saudi Arabia from the beginning is the revealing story.

Some power coming back in Louisiana after Ida. New York and New Jersey still under duress. Displacement galore. Visits by government officials do little or less.

Last night I read an article on a Jewish website where a select group of rabbis gave highlights of their High Holiday sermons. I'm always amazed how little rabbis have to say on their Biggest Days of the Year. No mention of Palestinians – or Israel for that matter. For most rabbis, Palestinians haven't existed except as foils. Support Israel is on their contract in bold print.

Somewhat new though, the absence of Israel. Has Israel become too controversial to be announced? Has Israel disappeared from their horizon?

The rabbis make mention of other issues. The pandemic is there. A mention or two of the new Texas abortion law. The overall theme is "coming home." As if gathering together in a formal setting rather than Zoom is, more or less, the essence of being Jewish.

I've asked myself often and again after reading the rabbis High Holidays layout: Is what rabbis present to their congregations what they believe? Or are they burying something deep inside they fear to share with their congregants? A curious Jew wants to know.

Yesterday, too, musing on my writing life. Have I given up on writing or have I written what I need to write?

I'm still writing my journal – evidently a need of mine – but my book length narratives are done, never to be revisited.

When I tell folks, who inquire about this turn, they hardly know what to think or say. Thank God I found painting.

Is it coincidence that painting appeared in my life at the same moment when my narrative writing disappeared? The meaning of this coincidence/turning is up in the air.

All of this came to mind yesterday when I received a message from a friend about Edward Said's airport delay just months before he died. Said had flown in from Portugal and was found to be suspicious by Customs. Baggage search and robust questioning ensued. After a while he was released.

The story triggered my last encounter with Said in Jerusalem – was it 2001? I bumped into him by accident as he and I were leaving the venue – in a basement corridor after his major address. By this time, Said was so sick he had been told not to travel and only to appear in public under extraordinary circumstances. Catching a common or odd germ could mean death. Said took his medical treatment quite seriously but was more liberal with his doctor's orders.

Lately in his lectures, Said had started referring to me as Rabbi Ellis. I became aware of this when, a few months earlier, I was listening to a recorded lecture broadcast by WBAI, the radical radio station in New York. I heard him almost by accident since I happened to hear his voice as I walked into my bedroom where the radio was on. As I entered by bedroom, I heard his distinctive voice preface a statement from me as written by "Rabbi Ellis."

This caught me by surprise since I had never suggested such a title anywhere and, of course, including to him. My first thought – Why does Said think I am a rabbi? Immediately after this thought, I felt a warning: I didn't want the Jewish establishment to think I was fraudulently claiming to be rabbi. I knew I had to advise Said of this but time was running out. I thought the time might be there in Jerusalem but when I saw his condition, I knew it wasn't going to be.

Then our surprise encounter in the basement.

After his lecture, Said was being hustled back to his hotel room by a number of handlers – there weren't to be any chance encounters. Said was a celebrity around the world, including and especially in Jerusalem. Everyone wanted to be near and be recognized by him. So when Said greeted me, holding his handlers at bay, I tried to dissuade him. Said wasn't to be constrained; he was determined to converse with me.

We chatted for a few minutes and toward the end of our encounter I simply mentioned my dilemma with him calling me a rabbi. I told him I knew it was out of respect for me and thanked him. Then I advised him that I wasn't in fact, an ordained rabbi. Said was taken aback – he apologized for his mistake. I told him that it wasn't important and not to worry, there were more important things to worry about, especially his health. Then something else unexpected happened. Said drew closer to me and exclaimed: "But Marc, you are a rabbi!" With that, he embraced me.

Later that night, as I was about to fall asleep, I thought to myself: "This evening, in Jerusalem, Edward Said 'ordained' me a rabbi."

Of all the strange twists in Jewish history. Said, the most famous Palestinian in the world, considered me as a rabbi. Could I ask for a more meaningful ordination?

My encounter with Said in Jerusalem triggered a series of questions beyond my person: What does it mean to be a rabbi at the end of ethical Jewish history?

Often, upon arrival at a speaking engagement, I have been greeted, and sometimes introduced, as Rabbi Ellis. At first I dissuaded the reference not wanting others to think I was passing myself as an ordained rabbi. When Said referred to me as a rabbi, I had to think again.

Does "rabbi" come with ordination only? Is "rabbi" only an official contractual designation? What are the needs of Jews in exile, Jews of Conscience, who live and witness for justice outside the institutional halls of modern Jewry?

After my "rabbi" encounter with Said, I went home and wrote a short essay with my first post-modern title: I Am/ Not a Rabbi. What does it mean to be a religious Jew who others, whether religious or secular, look for guidance. At the end of ethical Jewish history?

Said was very sick then and I wondered why he continued to travel and speak – quite frenetically – as he was dying. When I communicated this to the friend who messaged me, he remarked how Said fought for justice till the end.

I have other thoughts. I think they're related to the end of my writing life.

Since I published my first book when I was 26 and published book after book since – and remain an avid reader of books – the road away from writing is easier to note than to analyze.

When is it time to stop, slow down, retreat or retire from the scene? I have difficulty understanding people who can't let go, though I know letting-go isn't easy.

When do our commitments, highlighted in public, become performances for their own sake?

Ego is involved no doubt, though ego, properly directed, is important, a strong barrier needed to be out there, especially on controversial issues. The danger is confusing things, losing perspective and being out there in public as one's reason for being.

I love Said and he believed, quite rightly, that he could not be replaced. He hasn't been and won't. Still, my admiration for him is found somewhere else than the notion of dying with his boots on, which he did. For myself, though on such a comparatively minor stage, I shudder at the thought of this kind of end.

I've told my children that when my journey is at end, I want to be surrounded by books I have loved, my father's paintings and my own. I don't want the books I have written or artifacts of my public life close by.

I need to think through all of this. Or maybe it's better simply to embody my own sensibility – for what it is. After all, I am a person. Not a symbol. Not a cause.

Afternoon. After another short crossover walk. I'm still thinking through what I want to be surrounded by. As I prepare for my homecoming. And what I want and don't want near.

"Homecoming" is problematic for me. I first came across this term in my commentary on the murder of George Floyd and his funeral rites, a tradition I gather, in the African American community. I find homecoming lovely, endearing, probably ancient, but not for me.

Is death my return home?

My question for today is why I increasingly want to distance myself from definitions placed upon me by others, the well-intentioned and the not so well-intentioned. I don't even want messages from the few who speak or write about how important I've been to them.

Am I becoming cynical?

Perhaps these feelings are, at least partially, about my increasing suspicion of much of what I've been involved in. Which doesn't mean I or others have been wrong in speaking and acting for justice. I/we, with all our flaws and shortcomings, are on the right track. Yet this rightness as the sum and summit of our life is where I part company. That is and isn't me/us.

I want those accolades far from me. For what do they mean except a momentary bowing of the head in someone's direction. Before an email to be sent, a class to be taught, an outing, lunch or dinner for two?

The amount of trauma involved in speaking up and out – it's way too much to have things settled so easily. Away from the applause, life has to be lived. Why romanticize what I or others have gone through?

A long missive. Without conclusion. Right now. Perhaps forever.

Reading Gellhorn on love, yesterday and now. Also without conclusion. Gellhorn's paradox: In the process of shutting the door she leaves the love door wide open.

Here she is saying goodbye to a lover in 1945: "I think of you any number of ways; and I mistrust myself and I fear all this deeply. Because you see, you will fall more in love with me as I am more and more in love with you; I know this is so and unavoidable. And I will make a wonderful story about you in my mind, making you into many people you are not (as well as the person you are), and I will live with that story and count on it."

Gellhorn continues: "Meantime, you being more intelligent, will simply count on me. On what you know or understand of me, or on what you hope of me. I suppose love is like this: done with the most beautiful mirrors in the world."

Yet another Gellhorn goodbye letter in 1946: "And, beyond that, there is this dismal question of being in love, a phrase I handle with extreme caution as if handling six snakes and a live wire. For in the end, how do I know what love is, and where sex starts and ends, and love (for me always an operation done with the biggest fanciest mirrors in the world) comes true and is not my own invention, invention of need and loneliness and the terrible boredom of looking after oneself."

What to make of Gellhorn and her goodbyes? Just when things get closer than close she becomes suspicious. Mostly about her ability to survive what she wants.

Is there a greater good than giving it all away. If it isn't taken. Out of fear that the giving is a taking away?

Entering tonight the Jewish Big Days. Leading to the Big Day of Big Days. Except for the Big Days of Passover. Which holy days gives and takes away more?

Without forgetting – whether or not we are keeping score – the indigenous Jewish prophetic. The ultimate giver. And taker away.

Or forgetting Said and our encounter in Jerusalem.

DAYS OF AWE

SEPTEMBER 7

Rosh Hashanah. First light.

At the crossovers, visiting one then another. Then on the backroads with a short excursion onto the beach. This is what I have for now. Enough.

Rosh Hashanah's first light. Plain but pretty in its own way. May the New Year be good. And sweet!

First light is already old. Traveling from ancient times. Yet just arrived.

Like our High Holidays. Filtered, refracted. Redacted, edited.

Like our lives. Parts lost and found. Parts focused upon and rediscovered in a new key.

Light is what we have. Each morning. Each year. The piling on of history. Things in place. Hard to move. Years, generations, centuries.

Our ritual incantations. Liturgies that sustain and challenge us. As if the real isn't. As if our boundedness is an illusion. As if we are floating in another space. For those moments.

So how seriously to take New Years on anyone's calendar – and for Jews the Days of Awe, Yom Kippur up ahead.

The Day Without a Future. So I wrote some years ago. Named because of the lack of confessing the continuing injustice against Palestinians first and foremost. Yet the Day Without a Future keeps coming around the corner. As a reminder. Of.

Confessions are coming. Few but growing. With depth. Without depth. With history in mind. Without history in mind. Sorting out our confessions is the challenge of the days ahead.

Too late for sure. It may not have mattered anyway. Confessions in the winds of history. Who knows where they will land. If not where intended. Somewhere Else?

I wonder if I/we should drop the drama. Let the days come and go. Make them ordinary time. Which they are. Unless we make them extraordinary. If that could be done. In real time.

Holy days on our calendar. In our lives. Perhaps best to sit them out. On a cushion of one's choosing.

Surprise yesterday. A response to my Days of Awe painting. An invite tomorrow to Zoom into Union Theological

Seminary. Shall I make the same confession I made 30 years ago – in the same place? My (flickering) light returning.

My remuneration? The new biography of Edward Said. The perfect gift. My old companion returns to accompany me during these days.

Our companions define us. They mark our history. Our lives.

SEPTEMBER 8

Waking, 4:35, with many dreams, to greet the second day of Rosh Hashanah.

In my dream I visited a US embassy abroad. It was a small embassy, with a cemetery in front, just across a narrow street. In between the embassy building and the cemetery there was a helicopter landing pad. While I was walking nearby, a helicopter landed with the US ambassador aboard. Strange though, the helicopter, high-tech, landing in a small perimeter, touched down, flipped bottom to top and flipped back to land on its feet, so to speak. Hard to describe. Or figure out.

Last night I slept with my windows open. As I did in my pre-air-conditioned childhood, and now, when the weather turns cooler. This time it was a necessity – my AC is on its last legs. I can't complain since my AC lasted and worked well beyond its allotted time, the sea salt corrosion atmosphere and all. But replacements are expensive, especially with the new environmental regulations I support and barely afford them.

I did go out for first light. Crossovers and then on the beach. High tide it was, increasing the difficulty of my walk, but the sky was a pretty pastel blue with highlights of various colors throughout. I noticed a few surfers in the water. As I left the beach, a woman with a determined look hurriedly walked by me, a rosary dangling from her hand. She seemed to be in distress. I wondered if I should ask her if I could be of help.

I'm still taking it walk-easy but I'm determined to make it back to my Chapel of Love for Yom Kippur. Though I suppose Rosh Hashanah would have been more in tune. Yet the Chapel has also been my confessional. So both ends of the Days of Awe.

Yesterday was a full day. In the morning I Zoomed into Tzedek for Rosh Hashanah services. When Rabbi Rosen Zooms from his home, Torah studies and alike, the medium is quite good. When from the building where Tzedek holds its services, the Zoom is less favorable. The sound is more distant; it's like being doubly removed from those gathered live. This suits me fine in a way. Since distance from religious ritual allows a certain freedom. I'm able to hear the prayers and the sermon. I'm also able to move around my apartment – and paint.

I listened and painted during the service which, though quite traditional, is also innovative. Especially the prayers for justice. Hard to imagine many rabbis or congregations up for prayers for Gaza, for restorative justice, for an ecological turn around, for a Jubilee year where the prison-industrial complex is banned.

Yet – and this isn't anyone's fault. At the end of the day. It's more or less the same concerns every year. God doesn't act on our prayers. As a community and society, neither do we.

Yesterday, too, in preparation for my Zoom into Cláudio Carvalhaes's class at Union Theological Seminary, I rested in bed in the afternoon after the Rosh Hashanah service and thought of my last encounter with Edward Said – since I was going to start my presentation with that encounter – the encounter where he "ordained" me a rabbi.

Such a secular person Said was, why, then, was it important for him to think of me in religious rather than secular terms?

Years later, I still ponder this moment.

I was almost weeping, when I heard a package drop at my door. It was Cláudio's payment for my presentation. The new biography of Edward Said.

Before bed, I dipped into the biography. Not in a linear way as I usually read biographies. Rather I wanted to encounter Said in different parts of his life as I encountered him in life. To my delight I found from the start that the author, Timothy Brennan, a former student of Said's, had rendered Said's personality just as I experienced it – as a bundle of seemingly contradictory characteristics that, when observed, fit into a distinctive, irreplaceable intellect that came alive through a personality, an ambition and a boyishness that remains unforgettable.

So when I overcame my initial hesitancy in reading the biography, I became excited and thought of a lecture I'd love to deliver – "My Important Encounters with the Edward Said I Hardly Knew." It won't happen I know, since only elite luminaries are asked to lecture on Said. Nonetheless, my Said-take is different. Along the lines of Brennan. With a Jewish twist.

This morning I spent time with Cláudio's class with Edward Said in mind. Much to say about it once the dust settles. For now, I was too emotional for sure.

No matter how many times I speak about the end of ethical Jewish history my emotions run deep. I can't wrap my mind around our decline. Our thoughtlessness. Our violence. I will never accept it.

And I – we – are powerless to stop it.

After class I painted my encounter with Cláudio with the students, with Said, with myself. My therapy.

My confession was recorded. It may be sent around. It may be too strong to be viewed. We shall see.

Though I only said. What everybody knows.

Now, in the late afternoon, my morning encounter still pulses through me. What to do with my confession. Now 30 plus years old. Counting up rather than down. My confession will be with me forever. You can't travel Jewish without it. Can you?

Jews are still mired in our suffering. Without suffering. Any more than others. Often less. We still hold on. To.

But if everything in Israel against Palestinians is planned. Statecraft exercises, expansion grids, land theft, bureaucratic handling of it all, politicide – a civilian occupation it is. With guns galore. How long can you go to the Holocaust well. Without falling. Into?

What we didn't know, we didn't know. Now that we know enough or more, what to do? Without just letting it slide and championing what's easiest.

We are no worse. Not by a long shot. We are no better. Not by a long shot. But there has never been Jewish without the feeling of being different and, yes, better.

Even today our very own hawks and liberals keep on that "better" track. So that when some Jews and some others point the finger back at us we're startled. As if the finger pointers come from an unknown universe that harkens back to our darkest days.

Yes, of course, we are aware. Thus, the doubling down. Is our Holocaust trauma the past or our present? Perpetuated by our injustice? Caused now by others or ourselves?

To a comment from one of the Jewish students on my Cláudio Zoom, about compassionate listening of and between Israelis and Palestinians. Feeling one another's pain. I responded: "Revolutionary forgiveness begins with justice at the center. If you're abusing someone. Someone has to halt the abuse. Intervene. There will be time later to sort out trauma. Though power isn't always about trauma. If you respect Jewish. Stand up! Say it aloud. Shout it if you have to. Silence is not our friend."

SEPTEMBER 9

Waking. Day 3. The Days of Awe countdown.

The intensity of it all. Where does that intensity go when the countdown ends? Into the black holes of the religious calendar I suppose. The Jewish calendar moves with the moon. Do the black holes of the universe move with it? There must be a rabbi from long ago who thought so.

Synchronizing our lives and our religious calendars. Or, as an anarchist that I might be, at least religiously, can I move forward and backward, sideways, spiritually in and out as I please. This, without a community in real-time, arguing for Jewish in the broader arc.

First light was wonderful this morning. Many sky colors; different shades of orange and yellow against a pale blue sky. The tide fluctuated, at first high, then lower. I thought I might take a chance on my Chapel of Love. I did and made it. As the sun rose.

In the Chapel, I said my prayer, lingering on the lines where I thank God for waking me to this new day, making me a Jew and calling me to be free. As I left the Chapel, the sun was rising higher. Birds flew here and there. Surfers were riding the waves.

I came off the beach early, hoping to preserve my strength and rest my back. My walk home on the backroads was slow, almost a crawl. I was happy, though, that I made it back to the Chapel. Thrilled.

Thunder and lightning last night as I headed to bed – and quite humid it was. With the AC still on the brink, the atmosphere in my apartment has changed for the worse. Fortunately, I'm a fan person; my fans have saved me so far. And, as good luck, the rain continued through the night, cooling the air a bit.

Lots of dreams, only partially remembered. The most vivid was an encounter with an Asian American woman I've met only once in my waking life. We were at a conference seated together when she started lamenting the trafficking of Asian women and the black hole they fell into. We chatted for a while about the public discussion of trafficked women and commented on an Oprah Winfrey program we both had seen. Overcome with grief, she started to cry and asked me to hold her. Which I did. Then it was time to move to the next venue. I walked back to my assigned seat to gather my belongings but, with all the emotion, I lost my bearings. I couldn't find my way back.

Remembering yesterday's Union encounter. So intense. Too much. I think for my archives only. There's a limit to what people can take of me. A limit of what I can take of myself. Then morning arrives and I'm back in the saddle, so to speak. It's endless, more or less. A blessing. A curse.

Reading the biography of Said in the evening, with much to be learned. Some of it relating to me. Of note was Said's closeness to the British Jewish sociologist and philosopher Gillian Rose who Said felt "twinned" to. As Brennan relates, Rose's "command of philosophy impressed him deeply just as her uncompromising intellectual style – influenced like him, by Adorno, as well as by a great dislike of poststructuralism – was one he felt entirely his own."

Said's affinity for Rose may explain a mystery that remains with me since Rose's untimely death not long after I met her at, of all places, Auschwitz. It was 1992 and both of us were part of a delegation of intellectual and rabbis that went to Auschwitz at the height of the Carmelite Convent controversy. I was quite surprised when Gillian took the initiative and introduced herself to me. In my ignorance, I didn't know of her; it was clear, and to my surprise, that she was quite familiar with me.

There are deep similarities with my encounters with Said and Rose that I might explore another time. But what intrigues me about their connection is by way of my visit to Rose's university in the United Kingdom shortly after our encounter at Auschwitz. There I attended her seminar on Hegel, had lunch with her at the university and later had dinner at her home.

When I arrived at Gillian's home, she was saying goodbye to a quite emotional student. After he left, she took me to her den and pulled off the shelf my 1990 book, *Beyond Innocence and Redemption: Confronting the Holocaust and Israeli Power*. I wondered where she had come to know of the book but was too surprised to ask her.

I knew that Said had read my book cover to cover and thought highly of it. It was after reading the book and an article I published in the *Journal of Palestine Studies* that Said contacted me via letter. Said asked the *Washington Post* if he could review the book, a request they denied. Because of their "twinning" I think it likely now that Said alerted Gillian to my book.

Said was closer I think to Gillian's better-known sister, Jacqueline, whom I met briefly at a conference in London after Gillian's death. I also struck up a friendship with Gillian's mother after I wrote an elegy for Gillian in the London Tablet. For several years afterward, on speaking tours to the U.K., I stayed at Gillian's mother's home. We had late night sessions talking about Gillian and her last difficult days. Gillian's controversial writing in her last book deeply hurt her mother.

What a find! The connections Said made. And I did too. But mine were of a different sort, as one who was much lesser known. What to do with me, Said and Gillian must have thought.

Now I'm thinking that my relationship with Said and Gillian was quite similar. They discovered me; I watched them perform from a distance, even when close by. Indeed, they were both performers. Until their very end.

SEPTEMBER 10

Friday first light. Another pastel blue sky, with highlights. Calming during this intense week.

Shabbat begins tonight. Next week Yom Kippur. So we're in between the celebration of the New Year and Judgment Day.

Interim. Interregnum. Time to take a breath. In and out.

This morning I ventured to close crossovers and spent a short time on the beach. Yesterday I made it to my Chapel of Love without aftereffects. I don't want to push my luck though. I'll take it easy for the next couple of days.

September 11th – 20th anniversary – tomorrow. Lots on the news about it. What to do with religiously-inspired terror? And our co-religionists? Coming to grips with our religions, Judaism included, without excluding Islam and Christianity. As if those conducting terror in the same or different forms aren't really one of ours.

Buddhism and Hinduism as well. Hardly innocent.

"They" are ours. Is Benjamin Netanyahu not a Jew? Ariel Sharon? The ranks of the Israeli government. Army. Not Jewish? The Constantinian enablers of Israel's occupation of Palestine, the American Jewish establishment. Are they from a different religion?

As part of a people, even in opposition, I am responsible too.

Still hot inside. My AC guy is coming later this morning. I need a new unit for sure, but I hope he can do something to tide me over until he can install it. My AC guy is nice and honest, an independent businessman I trust. The last time he was here, though, I made the mistake of asking him how he was doing through the pandemic. His views on Covid are all mixed up. As we talked I realized he's a frustrated Trump supporter. So now I will stick strictly to the business side with him.

Though the days could be hotter, they're hot enough. Nights though are okay, at least for me. Florida summers are not recommended for the faint of heart.

I had no idea that this Yom Kippur season would feature the encounter of encounters with Edward Said but so goes life. The past is never far away.

Reencounter with Said is more like it. Where I try to understand what my encounters with him in real time were all about. The present is too busy, too full, mostly with extraneous junk, as you later realize. When things slow down the present then, now past, re-emerges.

What to do with memories so vivid they have a continuing life, perhaps an even stronger presence than when the encounter first happened?

Going through the Said biography right to the end yesterday. Dipping in. Skipping. A lay of the land read. With more to come.

Tidbits of interest:

1. Said's classic book, *Orientalism*, came about in the shadow of war(s). It began in the aftermath of the 1973 Arab-Israel war; the first draft was completed a year after Nixon's last bombing campaign in Indochina. Originally, Noam Chomsky and Said, who were already close associates, even friends, were supposed to write a book together. Due to other commitments, Chomsky bowed out. What arrived instead was Said's classic.

2. Brennan claims *Orientalism* was a mixed bag, a claim Said agreed with. Rather than a wholesale condemnation of the Western intellectual tradition, Said acknowledged a continuing debt to that tradition. This is one of the reasons Said had less and less interest in the field of Ethnic Studies he helped lay the groundwork for. In Said's view, the field had become too enamored with its representation of the traditions once defined negatively by the West. Even as most in the field benefitted from, and were intellectually indebted to, various Western traditions.

3. By the time I met Said he had already been diagnosed with the disease that ultimately took his life. It wasn't in evidence to those who encountered him the way I did. Only in the last few years of his life did his decline become obvious. Very much so.

4. Said wrote a lot – obvious. But Brennan notes his failures to complete projects he thought important. This included a novel he labored on for a long time and a major work on several philosophers he thought underrated or misunderstood. Said succeeded. He also failed.

5. In the biography, Said comes across – as I've always thought of him – as a consequential intellectual rather than a deep thinker. Said was a man in perpetual motion, striving to make an impact but also determined to keep his dominant place in the pantheon of international intellectual movers and shakers. Said could be boyish – his charm. He also had a significant ego.

6. Though Said was quite levelheaded even when he was on the offensive, as he often was, with the Oslo Accords all bets were off. Though Said often stated that Palestine wasn't a significant player in world politics, usually opting for a more universal sensibility, when he felt Palestine and Palestinians had been betrayed by their leadership, he was broken in half. It turns out, as I often thought, that Palestinian particularity was at the center of Said's life.

7. It is clear from the biography and my conversations and experience of him, that though quite open and gracious, with a dose of uncertainty about his accomplishments, Said was supremely sure of himself and his place in history. Said understood himself to be the supreme narrator of Palestine. He didn't envision a successor. In fact, his "successor" at Columbia University goes unmentioned in the biography.

There's more. Another "coincidence," like Said's encounter, and mine, with Gillian Rose? When I read that Said's *Orientalism* began after the 1973 war, known by Jews as the Yom Kippur war, again these days are markers in my relationship with Said. It brought back memories of my first visit to Israel in October 1973. Yes, I was in Israel for some weeks before and during the first days of the 1973 war.

I remember it all vividly. I was outside of Tel Aviv staying on a kibbutz when the war started. That day I was traveling with a few Swedes when the sirens sounded and, walking to our next stop, we saw residents in the apartment buildings across the street file quickly downstairs. My companions and I thought it was a fire drill; I remember marveling at the full response to such a drill. Some of the residents who saw us walking in the street waved to us and, when we didn't respond, they became emphatic. That's when we realized this wasn't a fire drill. As we approached the people they informed us of what was happening and we joined them in their air raid shelter. It was Yom Kippur. The war had begun.

I had gone to Israel on a dare of sorts from my Hebrew school teacher who, after visiting Israel in the wake of Israel's victory in the 1967 war, waxed eloquent about the marvels of Israel. Though I was mostly ignorant of Israel and the Palestinians, I had read about Palestinians in the aftermath of the war. I queried my teacher if he had met any Palestinians in his time there.

It was an innocent question; I was curious. When he responded angrily at the question, I was stunned. His clinching line set me off on my journey: "You don't know anything, you've never been there!" he said with a raised voice, almost shouting. As with any teenager that kind of assumed authority rankled. If I ever had a chance, I was determined to see Israel for myself.

So it goes. My Hebrew school teacher's love of Israel had unintended consequences with regard to me and, over time, with more and more Jews. The Yom Kippur war was a coming of age for Edward Said. And for me.

What I saw in Israel before and during the war was something that took me almost a decade to digest. The land of Israel – and Palestine – was indeed beautiful. It was also troubled. It seemed that Jews of European background, like me, were up. Palestinians of Middle Eastern background were down.

As an American Jew and a student of the Holocaust, I knew something was profoundly wrong. A great reversal was taking place. Had we, the too often persecuted and oppressed, become the persecutor and oppressor?

SEPTEMBER 11

Shabbat. September 11th. Waking, my field of dreams departed, as rain arrived.

When the rain subsided, I embarked on what I thought would be a short crossover excursion. The low tide and cool breeze lured me on. I made it back to my Chapel of Love.

The quiet there. Meditation time. I did say my prayer. After all, the Book of Life and Death is, according to tradition, opened wide during these days.

What a wonderful sky, light blue clouds cascading across the sky. I saw several guys on beach bikes, a surfer or two in the water. A couple with small children. Birds on the shore.

September 11th. Our turbulence – weather, terror, the routine functions of power. Is terror the exception or the rule? Albert Camus wrote of this long ago, the presumption of innocence masking culpability. That strange juxtaposition – "When crime dons the apparel of innocence."

Not in religions only. Far from it. Or rather that which is designated as religion. Modernity as the great world religion. We all bow to.

How destructive modernity has been, even with its wonderful promise of abundant life. We can't give it up. We may not survive it.

Modernity's promise is too seductive. To live beyond our means. With triage our unannounced mantra.

Life abundant for the few and far between.

Torah study this morning, the last before Yom Kippur. I will Zoom in and see what's going on. Like last week, I'll paint as I listen.

Rabbi Rosen is so open to questions it's hard to know what he believes. If belief enters into the textual equation.

True, with many rabbis and so different than Christian clerics. It's hard to discern the doubt pastors have, if doubt they have. Which they must, I think. If they doubt out loud perhaps they fear the entire tradition they represent will collapse.

Better to be silent?

Orthodoxy is a peculiar setup. We think of orthodoxy in relation to religious belief. It can be found elsewhere though. Modern Jewish orthodoxy? Once it was God, then Holocaust and Israel.

The fear of letting go of the powerful twinning of Holocaust and Israel leads to the ongoing Jewish Civil War between Constantinian Jews, Progressive Jews and Jews of Conscience.

Jews of Conscience are in deep, deep exile. With other People of Conscience, themselves in exile from their religious and political traditions, they find community in what I call the New Diaspora.

Lingering for a moment. Imagining Yom Kippur in the New Diaspora. The Days of Awe. Jews journeying with other exiles. To?

Is the New Diaspora. A journey together. Without a destination?

Most think our journey is toward justice. With the arrival date soon, if not tomorrow. Though the delay seems infinite. Like the Second Coming of Jesus.

Perhaps the New Diaspora will develop a creed. Like most other creeds such a creed would develop in empire, even as a form of resistance.

Creeds as danger zones. Lest the New Diaspora become an auxiliary to empire. My view: When dissent becomes part of the landscape of empire and its resistance becomes normalized, unintentionally, but functionally, dissent becomes part of empire's logic, a lever for its consolidation.

I hit the Said/Yom Kippur Wall yesterday. Too much intensity, even for me. I promised my journal I would continue writing until Yom Kippur. I will.

Writing the Yom Kippur Wall. On the Yom Kippur Wall. Through it.

Tunneling under the Yom Kippur Wall. Leaping over the Yom Kippur Wall.

Jumping down from the Yom Kippur Wall. Walking its length.

Dylan's All Along the Watchtower Wall. Israel's Apartheid Wall.

In all these years of writing about and speaking on Yom Kippur, it wasn't until yesterday that I connected the obvious; my first experience of Israel and Palestine was crystallized during the Days of Awe. The days before and during the Yom Kippur War.

It was October 1973 and I was on my own traveling through Israel and the newly occupied Palestinian territories. I was a tourist of sorts but one with an underlying mission of exploring my Hebrew teacher's "How dare I" mention Palestinians.

Mingling in the Old City of Jerusalem, when it was still Arab in population and culture, I felt I had entered a foreign place of being. The few Jews of European background I saw in the city looked out of place. I certainly felt out of place. Though Jerusalem was supposed to be my homecoming.

The Israeli and Palestinian youth hostels and homes I stayed at were different in Jerusalem and elsewhere. The Israeli hostels had a certain regiment, more like their European counterparts. The Palestinian homes I boarded at were friendlier, looser, for me, like places out of time.

The buses I traveled on were quite different, separate and unequal. The Israeli buses were new and air conditioned. The Arab buses were old, without air conditioning. The Israeli drivers were armed with weapons, as were the soldiers sitting among the other passengers. The Arab bus drivers and passengers were unarmed.

These were outward signs of the more structural differences I observed but couldn't quite name. It took me a decade or so to name them. I had no idea that my naming would be so controversial. After all, what I saw during my month-long journey couldn't be more obvious to anyone. So I thought.

My newly acquired Jewish education, as it were, deepened with my travel back to Israel and Palestine in 1984. This time I traveled among Palestinians with the intent on meeting those who had been defined as my Other. With a justice twist the following year, these encounters gave birth to my Jewish theology of liberation.

Even as I wrote, I searched for words to describe the sea change in Jewish history I observed. Rereading my words now, that struggle remains with me.

It shouldn't be simple to describe the end of ethical Jewish history. It isn't.

All of which brings me back to Said and Yom Kippur. With Said, I never struggled with words or ideas. There was about him a deep acceptance of me as a person and as a Jew – that was my experience with him.

Simply put, we trusted each other without a struggle. We did not have to build trust. That assumed trust allowed me to admire his charisma as something more than an egocentric intellect striving to stay on top of the heap.

Thinking yesterday as I closed my journal, what I hadn't yet broached in pondering Said – that Said was a consequential intellectual, much like Noam Chomsky, with neither being especially deep thinkers despite being, obviously, ace intellectuals. And that the charisma Said exuded, tied to time and place to be sure, was, in a certain way, the sign of a prophet. For what is a prophet if not one who carries and articulates the suffering and possibility of a people's history?

In my encounters with Said, I experienced this prophetic sensibility repeatedly. Palestinians who waited in line to meet him, each one with their particular story that exemplified the history of Palestine in one way or another, weren't being fooled.

Said was coy about this adornment, always informing me, as a colleague, that our exchange of ideas was more important than this ritual of meeting the one who narrated the story of his people. But I, standing to the side and often backing up and out of the scene, loved this devotional exchange. As Said, despite his demurrals, quite obviously did.

An example vivid in my memory: At a huge conference in Boston, I was with Said as a crowd gathered around him. Seeing the line and not wanting to interfere, I began to back away. As Said saw me disappearing, he reached out, grabbed my arm and, pulling me toward him, exclaimed: "Don't leave me now, Ellis!"

Vintage Said.

Yesterday I read a review of a recently released movie where the reviewer characterized the lead character as a "seductive force field." Reading this description, I thought of my experience with Said in Boston but also at an event in Chicago. Said had just returned from traveling to South

Africa where the apartheid regime was falling and knowing that Nelson Mandela would one day become President. Said was quite excited by his visit; South Africa was an example where justice in the face of great odds could be achieved. This was one of his first public events after his return.

Said entered the venue to a standing ovation; the crowd parted like an entrance scene in an old Hollywood musical. I stood next to Said as he went forth and wondered if I or any Jewish dissenter would ever be greeted in a similar manner by a crowd of eagerly awaiting Jews.

Surely Chomsky has been so greeted but mostly for his broad secular political critique of American power. On the theme of the Jewish tradition – and the indigenous Jewish prophetic – I couldn't then and can't now imagine such an embrace.

Though seductive force fields can move in different directions, for all his striving and ambition, his faults and failures, the sharp elbows thrown at him and those he threw at his critics, there was something about Said that centered and narrated the hope of his people. If he was holding out a hope that would never be realized and, if realized, would be tarnished as other hopes are, so be it.

What I witnessed in Chicago and in other encounters with Said was a deep yearning among Palestinians and an increasing number of Jews for what I described several years before Said's death as revolutionary forgiveness – forgiveness with justice at the center.

SEPTEMBER 12

Sunday. I awakened with a sense of heaviness. My mind was a bit cloudy, like a fog had settled inside me overnight. So I dressed and went out early for first light.

I started too early. It was still dark when I entered the beach. Along with my cloudy head, my legs felt heavy.

But when first light appeared, a band of orange on the horizon, with a low tide and a steady breeze, my mood and legs changed for the better. It wasn't the Day of Judgment after all. Deuteronomy could wait for later in the day.

Before me was the beauty of the world. I still had time to breathe in and out.

What to make of the Days of Awe disparity I experience at first light? A wayward Israel. A bellowing God. Moses on his last legs. My feeling of newness, even with an aging body. The day ahead. Wonder.

Without denying the brokenness within us and outside in the world. Suffering wherever it is. The abuses of power throughout the world. Our changing climate. Terror in all its forms.

Speaking of which, the September 11th programming yesterday was 24/7 as I expected. I didn't tune in for much. A great tragedy for sure. Its aftermath too. Wars galore.

9/11 was like a great prize falling into Israel's lap. At least for the Israeli government. As a fighter against terror, at least perceived as such, Israel was seen as holding that thin line between freedom lovers and death.

The terror industry that grew up within the wake of 9/11. The terror-industrial complex. A great engine of economic growth, looked at in a certain way. Billions upon billions allotted. Jobs galore. Political rhetoric ramped up. Dissent disqualified. The accelerated separation into us and them.

I Zoomed in yesterday to the last Torah study before the Big Day. Rabbi Rosen parsed Deuteronomy 31. A relatively short chapter as Torah chapters go. Hardly sweet. More dire warnings. To the max. A terror text set in ancient times.

In the text, we find Moses waxing eloquent on the secret message from God, now gone public. Moses isn't going to cross the Jordan into the Promised Land.

My God, I thought many years ago. What a raw deal! For Moses' sins – give me a break. When measured over against his leadership, stewardship, perseverance.

How well Moses served the Israelites. And God. The good advice Moses gave to God. Moses's willingness to deal with God straight-up. Moses befriending God. What better companion could God have than Moses?

So bad on God, in my view, unforgivable really. Unless God was saving Moses from the ultimate unraveling of the Israelites in the land. Since before and in this chapter, God's tidings are disaster ahead, disaster imminent, disaster, more or less, inevitable.

Like Israel's history was preordained for failure.

To be sure, God didn't see what many Jews see today – perhaps in light of the history of the modern state of Israel. That smiting this group and that group, the wholesale slaughter that Joshua is charged with doing, when God himself isn't taking charge.

A great injustice was done, for sure. To the Israelite Others. Who, by the way, the Israelites must have been very attracted to. Why prohibition after prohibition against mixing and matching, pairing off with the natives and their Gods, if the Israelites weren't willingly crossing all sorts of borders?

Deuteronomy 31. Language! Sure there is the choice placed before Israel, life or death. But the deck against Israel choosing life, as God defines it, is stacked against Israel.

Anyone reading the Torah text knows what's going on. Israel is going to fail; the Israelites are already charged with plotting against God.

So garnering my limited Zoom abilities, I raised my virtual hand to query Rabbi Rosen. Mixing the ancient and the modern, I rose to my occasion. "Rabbi, since already, before entry into the Promised Land, God knows Israel will fail. And since we are failing again now. With the end of possibility then, the end of ethical Jewish history now, please tell us – what gives?"

No doubt Rabbi Rosen knew what was coming since being in control of the futuristic Zoom Board is somewhat akin to being inside the Biblical Tent of Meeting. And having read some of my writing and considering me something of a mentor, Rabbi Rosen smiled as he nodded his head and conceded I asked a question needed to be asked. After confessing to being unable to answer my query in a definitive way, he offered what we could do – struggle with such questions while pressing onward.

What to do with the Torah, with Moses, with the Promised Land, with war and terror and rape? And charged questions like: If there are false Gods, are there true Gods? One God? Any God?

These unanswerable questions are, in Jewish life, mediated through the prophetic. In my view, at least for now, the prophets hold these questions in abeyance – while still moving. Or rather the prophets carry these questions. Within. While maintaining a vision. Of.

The universal is also assumed now. One God/One World. I'm an agnostic about this vision. Rather, it seems, at least for Jews, particularity holds, or should. For Jewish is the root of the global prophetic. From which other communities embracing the prophetic find their way.

Arrogant? Perhaps. A considered opinion, as it were. Central to my being in the world.

So what happens to the prophetic with the Jewish indigenous and Jewish particularity that nourishes the prophetic – in the New Diaspora? Where exiles from around the world gather in consciousness if not geographically. As if they're going home. One day.

The truth is that these exiles are not going home.

Does the inability for exiles to go home mean the end of each exile's tradition, the exile's grounding and thus their roots?

Jewish isn't alone in trying to figure this out.

Once the final exile is named. As difficult as that is to name. Since naming what everyone knows deep inside. That you can't go home again. Because once exiled, exiles wouldn't survive at home anyway. Is too painful.

The answer? Exiles have a new home. With their fellow exiles.

And while those who entered exile have their past to reject and draw upon, the children of exiles and their children, have less and less of that former home. Somewhere down the generational line exiles exist fully and only in the New Diaspora.

On what traditions, cultures and religious images will these fully exiled grandchildren draw on? Perhaps they won't be exiled at all, having been fully assimilated to the dominant culture. Or, for some, existing in between everything.

Diasporic is the latest circulating terminology. So many diasporas now. Not just Jewish. Of every nation in the world it seems. Gathering outside their native lands for every reason under the sun. People fleeing ecological, economic, political, religious and military disasters. The search for a better way of life or just to survive. Entire patterns of life and language changing. Now living elsewhere.

Is the New Diaspora made up of particular but interconnected diasporas?

Home sickness is real. Romanticized, too. Like the ancient Jews in Babylon, who longed for Zion, but held fast. Since the Promised Land was haunted. By God, tradition, religious authorities and corrupt politics.

Yet today, when most exiles can return home on a jet plane and don't, is diaspora real?

Whatever a certain generation feels for home, in the main, the next generation in general feels less. And their children even less. Where people are raised ultimately wins the day. As home.

For Jews, too?

An argued point. With many perspectives. Yet the fact that Jewish, always evolving to be sure, continues as it does, with losses and gains, such a small group population-wise, holding fast, is remarkable. Different.

The why and how of this persistence is argued, a many-sided journey. Yet the fact that Jewish survives throughout means something important.

When, some years ago, I was queried about this survival through the ages, with Jewish intact, I responded by simply suggesting: "Something happened at Sinai."

Of course, no one in their right mind would sign on to such a response. I'm certainly open to a better explanation. Or even a number of explanations to cover more bases. Since it's now unfashionable to speculate about essence, or even suggest essence as a possibility, I'll leave it at that.

As a Jew who knows that Jews, if not others, have always felt themselves to be different. And, with various definitions, of being exceptional, if not chosen among the nations. So that Jews have felt that other nations are, in fact, Other Nations, a definition no other nation need accept. The question remains for Jews in the New Diaspora: How to retain and nourish some sense of the particularity of Jewish?

Yet another issue in the New Diaspora is politics and the political and how the world that follows its own course is to be viewed, argued for, and against. Most Exiles of Conscience feel bound to their former communities in arguing for justice and rightly so. Yet too often justice seeking becomes the *raison d'etre* of exile life. Knowing though that, in the main, justice, while being worked on, rarely if ever arrives as struggled for, it seems that too often justice itself becomes the God exiles once felt dissatisfied with.

The world can become better on the margins, which is quite important for those on the margins; the world can become worse for those on the margins and beyond. Wholesale change, dedicating your life to that, is a personal devotion and should be treated and respected as such. It should not, I believe, become a communal creedal affirmation – in essence, a religion.

The New Diaspora is not apolitical. Nor can it become stuck in progressive or even radical politics as a way of life. What kind of diverse politics it will have is up for discussion and, no doubt, debate. A lockstep approach won't do.

SEPTEMBER 13

Waking, too early, wide awake, hoping to close my eyes again before heading out. The forecast is for a low tide morning, so I hope to make it to my Chapel of Love. But as I write, I hear rain falling and thunder close by.

I did make it out and all the way to my Chapel of Love. Along the way first light was beautiful. Dark blue clouds forming within an opening white space.

What would I do without first light guiding me along the way?

In the distance two cruise ships were coming into port. Several others waited their turn. A submarine came out of port a few minutes later. It's the second day in a row, I saw one. Maneuvers, getting ready for the deep dive.

No Days of Awe beach markings but I noticed a giant Cross etched in the sand as I approached my Chapel.

Like voting venues, I want religious symbols to be at least a hundred feet from the Chapel. My Chapel of Love is open to all. No religious symbols allowed!

Home for breakfast and the news. Yesterday former President George Bush, hardly my favorite, launched an attack on the Trumpians and the Capitol insurrectionists, claiming they're cut from the same cloth. They need to be opposed. An astounding speech it was, though he could use a Yom Kippur confession booth or two for his own cut cloth.

How about a special reserved 24/7 confession marathon booth for our former President(s). With tight security provided, of course.

Yesterday word that my friend may be joining me for Yom Kippur. Plan is for him to arrive in the morning to help me with some chores and food shopping to prepare for breaking the fast at the end of Yom Kippur. We're in discussion about our schedule and how we'll modify the holy day expectations to make Yom Kippur our own time, too.

The Constantinian Jewish community wants a one-size-fits-all Yom Kippur fast – without a meaningful confession. Our Jews of Conscience fast is too late for our confession to turn things around. I'm an agnostic on full day fasts or similar calls from religious authorities of all stripes, even when I sometimes agree with them on other matters. Maintaining distance is crucial even when in agreement. Hypocrisy is everywhere. The best laid religious authority plans need adjusting, if not resisting.

Countdown to Wednesday night. Thursday. Serious business needs a personal touch.

I Zoomed in yesterday for Union Theological Seminary's opening ceremony. What a tradition. If I heard correctly Union is now 185 years old and counting. It is still going strong, with its added air-space Condo Tower multi-million-dollar revenue boost of recent vintage. I haven't seen its latest addition. It must be something to behold.

Union seems to be twinning with Jewish Theological Seminary across the street. They, too, have an air-space financial Condo Tower multi-million-dollar boost on tap.

Twinning radical theology and corporate capitalism. Is there any other way to go?

At the Union celebration, Cornel West was the keynote speaker, as he has returned once again to Union. You have to love Cornel. I certainly do. As a Christian he sees everyone in their quest for justice as "our" quest. Inspirational he is. Black gospel preaching in a new key.

I have an interesting history with Cornel stretching back to a joint appearance in New York City as my Jewish theology of liberation was hitting the streets.

I can't remember the date exactly. Probably late 1980s. I spoke, he responded. I remember Cornel as being supportive of my theology but somewhat guarded. Cornel was on the upswing but, as yet, relatively unknown. He was already in his trademark black attire, though, and after our event I remember driving with him in his last legs car. I was teaching at Maryknoll at the time. Perhaps he was taking me to Grand Central station to catch my upstate train.

I've had other encounters with Cornel including when he made a presentation in my honor at the American Academy of Religion in its 2011 annual gathering. His words were so beautiful I felt like weeping. I did.

Last night, I painted as I listened to Cornel speak. My title: "Cornel's Altar Call – For All."

Yes, of course, when I think of Cornel, I remember his recently deceased counterpart and sometimes rival, James Cone, who I first encountered in the 1970s, and often in the 1980s. These were the years when Cone was the real deal Black Christ or bust. What a competition between those two giants. Of who would captain the Black Theological Revolutionary Struggle ship.

Being so different, over the years they converged. More stories for another time but I'm so grateful I encountered both West and Cone up close and personal.

As Yom Kippur draws near, with Said, they accompany me too.

Thinking of Said and West and Cone, is Yom Kippur defined today by the Jews – and the non-Jews – who accompany us on Yom Kippur?

Who Constantinian Jews bring along with them. To Yom Kippur.

Who Progressive Jews bring along with them. To Yom Kippur.

Who Jews of Conscience bring along with them. To Yom Kippur.

Which group brings Who. Which group excludes Who.

Our Yom Kippur's Who's Who. Yom Kippur broadened. Redefined?

The myth of Jews retreating into isolation on Yom Kippur. We bring our lives and our personal and political companions along. Those whom we embrace. And oppose. Our allies. Our enemies. Those who enable us. Those we're at war with.

Christians, too. Do they worship alone on their holy days? Who accompanies them? Who's included? Who's excluded?

Holy Days as our engagement with the world. By other means. With our solidarity, our warfare, and everything in between.

Power isn't an intruder on our holy days. It's right in front of us. Where we are on the power index surrounds and defines us.

Musing too much on the religious calendar. Perhaps.

I think such musings are an unintended consequence of Israel's occupation of Palestine, where Jewish history is put to the test. Just like my meditations on God are the unintended consequence of Holocaust theology's argument with, if not denial of, God. That highlighted the possibility of God.

Lesson: You never know where history and reflections about the meaning of history, might take us. Sooner or later.

Though the prophetic was already deep inside me, through the Holocaust and Israel, I was pressed to confront both. Would this deep engagement with the prophetic have happened to me – and so many Jews – if Holocaust and Israel hadn't been offered to us as a demand of faith?

There's no question of the Holocaust or Israel's occupation of Palestine being a place of gratitude. Perish the thought. Yet in every generation, the covenant must be approached and embodied. That approach and embodiment take place within the context of tradition and the times in which we live.

The prophetic, for Jews, for so long, was projected outward on the non-Jewish world of power. The outward prophetic came home in my lifetime.

What would have happened to Jewish without the Holocaust and Israel as formative events in contemporary Jewish history? And what would these events have meant if not against the backdrop of the Jewish tradition?

The historical backdrop is so dramatic a reckoning had to take place. But to be in the middle of it all, where everything is on the line and decisions have to be made. Where does our community stand? Where does each individual stand?

Lots of pressure. Trauma. Opportunity. The need to find our own voice.

Jews of Conscience are in the middle of a Jewish Civil War with Constantinian and Progressive Jews on the other side, a war without end. The Jewish Civil War led to the exile of Jews of Conscience from mainstream Jewishness. I doubt there's a way home.

Is the exile of Jews of Conscience the last exile in Jewish history?

Image: Jews of Conscience walking into exile carrying the covenant with them.

Another image: Constantinian Jews attending Yom Kippur services with Star of David Helicopter Gunships guarding the Ark of the Covenant.

What is the meaning of these and other images of difficult hope and deep despair that have come my way during the last decades? What have these images said to me on previous Yom Kippurs? What will they say to me this Yom Kippur? What do these images say to us about the future of Jewish life?

Does the squandering of our ethical witness forfeit the long struggle of Jews throughout history to survive and flourish, while being a witness to ourselves and to others?

Traveling Jewish, I've found a deep hunger in the world for the tradition that has carried the prophets to stand up for justice and to turn the prophetic critique inward, as it was born to do. But, as well, to give strength to those outside Jewish, as an example.

The prophetic had to turn again, to return to our indigenous.

Teshuvah. To return. Repent. Turn away from. Toward. The great call of Yom Kippur. Found throughout in the prophets.

Did Edward Said ever attend a Yom Kippur service? So far the biography doesn't mention such an occurrence.

Once on tour in the U.K., I attended an Anglican service where "the Jews" were mentioned in the Gospel reading in a negative way. Of course, this and every Christian service is filled with and haunted by Jews, Judaism, Jewish history and Christian history toward Jews, too. After the service the female priest talked to me about how anxious she was with me in the congregation. She was forced to think about Jews in a different way.

Imagine living Jews in attendance when the Christian ritual is about certain perceptions of Jews by those who broke off from Judaism and used Jewish for their own purposes. Now think Edward Said at Yom Kippur services. Arriving and sitting with Jews on the Day of Judgment. At a typical synagogue where support for Israel is featured or is deflected by citing both sides as (possibly) desirous of peace. Or even at Tzedek where Palestinians are supported full throttle and invited to speak.

Instead of Said alone, what would a community of Palestinians in every synagogue, on Yom Kippur, mean for our Yom Kippur confessions?

Invite Cornel West, too. He's speaking a lot bolder about Palestinians now than when I first met him.

SEPTEMBER 14

Last night, writing before bed. The end of the Days of Awe drawing near. Before God, I have more to say. So waking here's where I was before I entered dreamland:

Theology as confession rather than affirmation of God's presence, majesty, omnipotence. Or God's absence, smallness, impotence.

It seems counterintuitive. It may be. But when the prophetic is at play in its indigenous state, God is no longer at the center. Sometimes God goes unmentioned. Assumed?

The prophet carries the question of God in her backpack, so to speak. Close at hand – under control. Close at hand – hard to get to.

God isn't at Central Control. The remote link is spotty. Once called, the prophet is mostly on his own. Neither omnipotent nor impotent, the prophet is steady as she goes.

When not on the run. Theologies make little sense if the theologian isn't in the midst of controversy. Like the Torah itself, theology is always moving toward or away from the prophetic.

Is the prophet the confessor of sin for Jews rather than God?

Jews in the prophetic tradition – so natural for Jews. With the prophets in exile – so natural for Jews. Should I be grateful that for Jews, the prophetic and exile are our home?

Home turf. We think comfort and contentment. Though as a Jewish poet once commented, home is also a most dangerous place.

Thinking now of Yom Kippur as a day of confession. Should all Jewish theology today be centered on confession? To the Palestinian people for justice denied and to Jewish history for the witness we have squandered?

Now this morning, up too early, before my walk, continuing:

Yom Kippur as mourning. Jewish theology as mourning?

All of my writing, whatever power it contains, is about loss. How else to describe loss but through confession.

As for repentance. With justice restored, perhaps one day, when it's too late. What had existed, what had been built up, will not be regained or rebuilt.

Confession: Theologies of liberation are clarion calls for justice. They're optimistic. God, the people, will pull the oppressed through. Looking back but unbeknownst to me then, my Jewish theology of liberation shunned the optimistic view; neither God nor the people will pull the oppressed through.

Though I didn't know what would happen in the next 30 plus years, one feels the trajectory in my writing – the worsening of the Palestinian situation and the growing militarization of Israel. What to do except, even in forward movement, mourn and confess that what needs to happen, most probably won't.

My Jewish theology of liberation was already a confession. That had no destination. There wasn't going to be a turning toward. The oppression of Palestinians will not be reversed. What we squandered is gone.

What I didn't know was how much longer it would all go on. And how much more squandering would occur.

I wrote then – there is still time. Did I believe that or was that a bone tossed. To keep hope alive?

Home now after a short crossover and beach walk. I'm still mixing it up – long haul, short haul. When I don't get to my Chapel of Love though, I feel like my desire is unfulfilled. I'm also trying to be patient so I don't have a back muscle strain recurrence. Balancing stability and desire. Lifelong work.

Before breakfast. Continuing my meditation:

Theology as confession. Also as the reduction of cognitive dissonance. The religious calendar as well.

What the religious calendar assures us will happen doesn't happen. Aspirational for sure, though, even the holy days that ostensibly save us and vanquish our enemies and promise salvation of one kind or another. The Yom Kippur choice of choices – to be written in or out of life. Hardly believable, even as metaphor.

Perhaps my Jewish theology of liberation was my way to reduce the cognitive dissonance I felt about Jews being good and what Jews were actually doing. Since if I had believed such behavior possible, what then?

I remember my encounters with Rabbi Irving Greenberg, the Orthodox rabbi, who writes so hauntingly about the Holocaust and attempts to reduce the cognitive dissonance of Jews toward Israel's crushing of the first Palestinian uprising. In 1988, Greenberg wrote a pamphlet titled, 'The Ethics of Jewish Power.' Arguing that when Jews didn't have power we could afford the prophetic, but now, having assumed power, Jews are undergoing the "difficult process of normalization."

In this process, Jews can no longer hold ourselves to the highest behavior. Since the lesson of the Holocaust is that Jews cannot afford powerlessness. Assuming power, so necessary, Israel, with the support of Jews worldwide, will likely cross ethical lines we condemn in others. For Greenberg, a sign of maturity is staying steady: accept the mistakes, work to minimize them.

The idea that we as Jews will act completely like others, though, is foreign to Greenberg. We can still act better than the Other Nations, even if the percentage of better behavior diminishes. In a classic case of the reduction of cognitive dissonance, Greenberg parses the difference Jews should expect of Israel.

Reading Greenberg as a Jew, while allotting for imperfection in empowerment, I held my breath and waited for the percentage difference. Would it be 80%? 50%? Greenberg's startling conclusion, while still holding fast to Jewish exceptionalism, was much less – 20% or even less!

Greenberg leaves the precise percentage of better behavior unmeasured. His point, though, is clear: Jews need a state where the margin of sinful behavior – something Jews have to get used to – allows the Jewish edge in ethical argumentation to be maintained. This necessitates another part of the difficult process of normalization – the diminution and, in some cases, the banishment of the prophetic from Jewish life.

For Greenberg, each Jewish generation has sins punishable by excommunication. For our era in Jewish history that sin is intentionally or unintentionally undermining Jewish empowerment in Israel. Lest, according to Greenberg, we be thrown back into another Holocaust reality. As for many Jews, after the Holocaust, Rabbi Greenberg feels the choice is power or mass death.

Now thinking, if we fast forward to Yom Kippur, were Greenberg to know of Tzedek's unabashedly anti-Zionist platform, repentance on Yom Kippur would mean disavowing Israel's very reason for coming into being. After all, Tzedek takes on the reduction of cognitive dissonance in the Jewish world by confronting it with a stark, and for Greenberg, thoroughly unacceptable, alternative.

Memory: Welcoming Rabbi Greenberg to my Institute for Justice and Peace at Maryknoll in 1988 where we were celebrating the life and work of the Peruvian father of Latin American liberation theology, Gustavo Gutierrez. After Rabbi Greenberg addressed the conference, we took a walk on the beautiful grounds outside. I had just returned from traveling to Israel-Palestine which was in the middle of the Palestinian Uprising. Catalogued in Palestinian and Israeli human rights reports was the Israeli torture of Palestinian prisoners. In turn, I had written about these reports, some of which Rabbi Greenberg had read.

As we were walking, Rabbi Greenberg asked me if what I had written was true – that Israeli soldiers were torturing Palestinians. I told him that both Palestinian and Israeli human rights groups had reported this and that even the US State Department had done so. Still finding it difficult to believe, Rabbi Greenberg paused and asked me if I thought these reports of torture were accurate. When I told him I did, he was silent.

In the silence, we continued walking for a few minutes. I felt a tension that wouldn't – couldn't? – be resolved. What did Rabbi Greenberg's silence mean, I remember wondering. I was ready for the response that never came.

Then it was time for him to depart. We shook hands. Rabbi Greenberg was gone.

Late morning. Closing in:

I hadn't thought of it then but wrote of it some years later, that with languages of all kinds, once the people who speak a language commit injustice, their language is used to name and deflect injustice itself. I realized this with regard to Hebrew when reading a Jewish philosopher analyzing the German language before and during the Holocaust. His conclusion, now in my words, was that the German language had become infected with atrocity.

> *The translation to present day Jewish life was easy for me, though haunting. That Hebrew, which through most of its history existed on the margins of state power, its speakers often being oppressed by and resisting that power, in becoming the language of the Jewish state, assumed the burden of power over Palestinians. And since the injustices committed against Palestinians and the torture I discussed with Rabbi Greenberg was ordered and carried out in Hebrew, Hebrew had itself become infected with atrocity.*

On Yom Kippur, Hebrew is the language we address God. And the rabbis who lead these prayers are either Israelis whose mother tongue is Hebrew or, for us here, rabbis who learn Hebrew in Israel.

Sobering. Our appeal to God on Yom Kippur is in the very same language used to torture Palestinians.

SEPTEMBER 15

Up and out to my Chapel of Love. Low tide morning. Calm. The lull before the confessional storm. Starting tonight.

Before leaving, scrolling, an old friend, a Maryknoll priest, posted a video of a dedication ceremony of Maryknoll's new solar panel array covering the parking lot I used when I taught at their school of theology. It's quite something – innovative.

What if the Catholic Church took its vast properties and, for God's sake, retrofitted them. For the New Diaspora?

Strange coincidence that I was writing yesterday of the Gustavo Gutierrez summer session where, among many others, Rabbi Greenberg spoke. I remember now another dimension to my Rabbi Greenberg story, so relevant to the sea change in Jewish history and Yom Kippur.

It occurred at a Holocaust conference in London that Rabbi Greenberg and I attended just weeks earlier in the summer of 1988, in the middle of the Palestinian Uprising. Considering my support of Palestinian freedom, it was amazing I was invited to speak at the conference. When I encountered Rabbi Greenberg there, the first time we met, he seemed upset with me. He thought I misquoted him in my writings on a Jewish theology of liberation. I was horrified at the possibility. Immediately after our encounter, I rushed back to my room and looked through the pages where I quoted him. I breathed a sigh of relief. The quotes were accurate.

Initially at stake was his commentary on the Sandinista revolution in Nicaragua and the recent stationing of US missiles in Europe. Rabbi Greenberg was mostly negative on the Nicaraguan revolution and mostly positive on the assertion of American power in Europe. These were just two examples of a larger question since Rabbi Greenberg thought himself a liberal, as in main the Jewish community was, at least in its sense of identity. What I found in Greenberg and other Jewish leaders was a neo-conservative drift, mostly due to an increasingly Israeli-centric world view.

If you want the US to fund Israel and be its protector, you can't have Jews on the Left protesting American imperial power. And if protests like that continue, the organized Jewish community has to be a counter-voice. The choice was there to be made. It was.

Rabbi Greenberg and the Jewish community had changed without adjusting their sense of identity. We were no longer who we thought ourselves to be. My Jewish theology of liberation pointed to this shift in bold ways.

Memory: At Maryknoll, Rabbi Greenberg was greeted with great respect, but I realized as he spoke that he had little idea of the liberationist pulse of the conference. So when he started speaking about Nicaragua – a focal point of solidarity with the group – he entered dangerous terrain. When he moved into even more perilous waters, I had to act quickly.

I stood and apologized for the interruption, noted that the hour was late and that Rabbi Greenberg's ride back to New York City would be arriving soon. I asked the conference participants to thank him, which they did, and offered the hope that Rabbi Greenberg would come again so we could learn more from him.

When we left the building, Rabbi Greenberg commented that his ride wouldn't be arriving for a half an hour or so. I looked at my watch and apologized for my mistake. How could I explain to him that he was digging a huge hole for himself and that I had rescued him from a discussion he wouldn't have understood? That is when our discussion on torture in the language of Hebrew took place.

Yesterday, strange or par for the course of my writing, when I come to the end of what I assign myself, I write more rather than less. I do not experience empty very often. There is always more to come.

So last night it was the same as the night before, thinking of my mourning for the end of ethical Jewish history and of Hebrew, our sacred language, having become the language of empire, now and forever infected with atrocity.

When our language mimics the languages of the Other Nations you become one among Others. Our protest notwithstanding.

So it goes with my writing this Yom Kippur.

I think of my journal days as dispatches from the New Diaspora – not the old diasporas, Jewish or those newly configured ones. And not with the attempts to recreate diaspora thinking, Jewish or otherwise, as if the old, being no longer and having once gestated over many decades, centuries and beyond, can be born anew. Illusions. No way!

And so while I interact and confront Rabbi Greenberg's "difficult process of normalization," I also disassociate myself from new forms of Diaspora Judaism. And a too easy anti-Zionism, depending on the definition one has, since there's so much ambivalence about Jews all around the world. To place ourselves in the hands of others is dangerous.

For Jews there's no going back before the Holocaust and Israel, with all both have meant. There's no going forward without them either. The great majority of Jews now live in the United States and Israel; this concentration will grow in the coming years.

For the first time in recorded memory most Jews live – and thrive – within empire. This is another sea change in Jewish history. Considering our history, Jews would be crazy to give up this privileged status, no matter its dire ethical challenges. And most Jews, including those who are critical of the Jewish assumption of power, except in rhetoric, will not give this status up either.

I am part of the New Diaspora. I am not a Diaspora Jew.

This is significant far beyond me. Those who claim Diaspora Jewish status. Aren't Diaspora Jews. They are Jews thriving in empire and, no matter their dissenting views, are protected by that which they criticize.

We have to be honest about our situation, with all its complexities, if we are going to face each other, face others and face God on Yom Kippur.

The Jewish Civil War among Constantinian Jews, Progressive Jews and Jews of Conscience is an internal one: How we are going to orient our lives in empire?

Despite our intentional outreach with those on the margins, we are not, as a community, changing places with anyone else. Truth be known, if those on the margins rise to privilege, whatever their intentional outreach, they won't trade places with others, including Jews, either.

Yom Kippur as a holy day, the Days of Awe themselves, while rooted in the Torah, are liturgically framed by the rabbis. Even more so, with the waning of the Rabbinic framework, they primarily serve as Jewish identity markers. For these reasons, the Days of Awe have lost much of the vitality they once possessed.

Yom Kippur, especially, is lost in a space only accessible, or mostly so, to calls of Jewish renewal, which have more to do with religious and political movements outside Jewish life than within it.

The hollowing out of Yom Kippur. If you're not going to make the Big Change, a True Turning. Why bother?

Yom Kippur as dress-up. Last night at the Metropolitan Museum of Art, for a big gala, Alexandria Ocasio-Cortez wore a high fashion dress. With lettering, big and bold, in red: "Tax the Rich."

When synagogues roll out their Yom Kippur red carpet perhaps there should be dresses with lettering: "Free Palestine."

So it goes. Or doesn't. Another year of nothing much. Even the very few synagogues featuring Palestinian voices are growing hollow.

Of course, it goes without saying, that during the Days of Awe, especially on Yom Kippur, Palestinians in Jerusalem and the West Bank are under Israeli lockdown. I doubt there are more severe measures for Gaza though. Could there be anything more severe than their daily – seemingly eternal – lockdown?

Looking back on my first visit to Israel-Palestine in 1973, I experienced a similar lockdown within Israel. When everything public crawled to a halt during the Days of Awe, I was stranded, in of all places, a small youth hostel on the Sea of Galilee. There were only two of us at the hostel and the accommodations were simple. My room had a bunk bed. I slept in the bottom bunk, my roommate slept on top.

My bunkmate was a mechanic who worked for the now defunct airline, TWA. He was on furlough. Since we were going to be together for a week or so, we exchanged names and a bit of our backgrounds. In the evening of the second day, he leaned over my bunk from on top and asked if I knew of Our Lady of Fatima; he was a devotee. No, I had never heard of her, I told him, whereupon he handed me a pamphlet and began relating what I considered one of the strangest stories I've ever heard.

Stranded during part of the Days of Awe in Israel, on the sea where Jesus walked on water – I learned this from the hostel brochure – and with a devotee of Mary – I quickly realized this was going to be a long week.

Three or four days later, a bit earlier than I expected, I was thrilled to escape from the Sea of Galilee and my Fatima-obsessed companion. As I celebrated, though, I was about to be stranded again.

The Yom Kippur war had begun.

Now, sundown, the beginning, the Kol Nidre service is about to begin. I have my Zoom ready and await my login information. We shall see how much I tune into the services. For sure I'll watch the Palestinian – African American speakers in the afternoon to see what hope can be spun. I now have the title and the names – "Restoration and Reparation from US to Palestine: A Yom Kippur Conversation" featuring Noura Erakat and Taurean Webb.

My friend will be arriving soon. I don't know if I'll write on Yom Kippur or write after it's all over. I've loved writing epilogues to my books – why not for Yom Kippur? As if, when finished with unraveling what I tried to understand, I'm ready for another departure.

Departure to where? Having dispensed the hard labor, I'm ready to fly. Yom Kippur is different, though. Instead of arriving new, I feel it a relic from another age, which was already on its last legs when I was a child.

How much battering can our holy days take before they're put to bed for good?

Nevertheless we hold on, seemingly, for dear life. Fearing even emptier days ahead.

SEPTEMBER 16

Waking a little after 3AM. Yom Kippur is here.

Wondering about the prophets:

Are the prophets our first light in the darkness?

The prophets don't gather others. They're singular.

The prophets speak loudly at times. Other times in secret.

The prophets perform in public. Also behind the scene.

The prophets speak to history and a people. They aren't looking for converts.

Whatever the prophets thought at first about their mission – doomed or destined to succeed – quickly they realize they are fated to negotiate what won't come to pass.

Yesterday my friend arrived a little after noon. We chatted as he helped me with a wash at the laundromat up the road. Three big loads it was, including a winter comforter that's been on the bed far too long. I'm looking forward to cooler weather.

Later we cobbled together a nice dinner for us and shared a beer. I put some finishing touches on a Yom Kippur painting with lots of green so far. Not as dark as I thought it would be. I'll see where it is when the sun rises.

The Zoom email I received from Tzedek only listed today's services. There's no mention of last night's Kol Nidre service which, through a fellow congregant, I learned was happening in real time. I found out too late. It was already midstream into the service. I was informed though that Rabbi Rosen's sermon focused on Palestine and the Jewish community's continuing inability to confront our enablement of injustice. Apparently, Rabbi Rosen was in good form. You have to admire Rabbi Rosen for speaking truth to power. I certainly do.

Earlier in the day, I received a Facebook message that my short essay on Yom Kippur from a few years ago is circulating again. Published in my Mondoweiss series, *Exile and the Prophetic*, the message features a photo of Abraham Joshua Heschel teaching a seminar. It's a wonderful picture of a great Jewish theologian and activist for justice.

I began the reflection with my encounter with Heschel, as an undergraduate, in 1972, just months before his death. A cherished memory it is. A survivor of the Nazi terror, who lost many relatives in the Holocaust and was, understandably, a supporter of Israel, what would Heschel say, pray and confess this Yom Kippur?

I remember sitting at Heschel's feet at a reception after his public lecture. Gathered with me were five or six students. Heschel looked tired and a bit irritated. When one of the students asked him about an issue in Jewish life, Heschel admonished him in a grandfatherly way: "I have written about this in several of my books. You should read them."

Rubenstein, one of Heschel's former students, was nowhere to be found that night; nor had he publicized Heschel's appearance. I understood that they had a falling out, a big one, over Rubenstein's writing on the Holocaust, especially Rubenstein's claim that in the Holocaust, God's covenant had been irreparably broken. Heschel had an argument with God; he couldn't abandon God. Rubenstein didn't deny God's existence. He simply couldn't accept a God who allowed the Holocaust.

The bitterness of it all. The Jewish Civil War didn't start with Israel.

If he were alive today, would Heschel confront Israel and its enablers full throttle – we Jews but also others in American political and religious life? Would he just lay it out as he did on race during the Civil Rights era?

In a back and forth on my Yom Kippur reflection, I found several strong comments. The strongest are defiant refusals to fast this year – the complicity of the Jewish community is too much. One of the defiant is religious, the other secular.

Yet another invoked Isaiah 58. So I went back and reread the passage. On the back of an envelope I wrote:

Isaiah is scorched earth. On fasting: How dare you!

The indigenous Jewish prophetic. Say it out loud!

Isaiah's fate. Sawn in half. Apocryphal?

The fate of the prophets. The persistence of the prophetic.

How to explain, then and now. That long straight line. Through history.

Does God love the prophets. On Yom Kippur?

God's name (for me): I AM WHO LOVES THE PROPHETS.

So I wrote.

A most difficult love. To believe in. It isn't a faith, though. That which can only be embodied.

Embodying the prophetic. Is it chosen? Given?

For the prophets of every age. So many misadventures!

Though we missed Kol Nidre and Rabbi Rosen's sermon, I hope to catch up on the details in the days ahead. Instead, we had our initial Yom Kippur discussion. The topic as it unfolded – committed thinking and writing as a "devotional practice."

First, I flashed back on the sacrifice and fulfillment of such a life. Then we flashed forward on a life as a committed Jewish thinker and activist.

What is worth confronting and how? What is worth sacrificing and to what purpose?

What should parents ask of their children? What should parents protect their children from?

Walter Benjamin wrote that the fuel of revolution isn't the hope for liberated children and beyond but the memory of enslaved ancestors. Was Benjamin right and can a father propose that for his own children?

A deep Yom Kippur encounter it was. We sat side by side. Not virtual.

In the morning we embarked on a sunrise walk. Strange it was for me to be walking with another person on Yom Kippur, Day of Days.

Solemn it isn't with him though, as we laughed at the quirks that come with age. My stopping at a bench to retie my sneakers as a precaution so they don't come untied on the beach. My slower pace, even though I've picked up quite a bit over the last months. My comments on people's beach outfits and assorted items they carry. Like the guy who carries an umbrella as he walks in case it rains. Or the woman who starts out just before sunrise wearing a jumper and, ten minutes later, has to shed and carry it for the duration because, with the sun, the heat arrives.

We did make it to my Chapel of Love. My friend was patient with me when I rejected this photo and that photo because of the way I appeared. I don't hide my age but, as I've noticed that with age and my early Parkinson's comes a masking in the face. Some of the photos made it look like I don't have much longer to live. I don't feel like I sometimes look.

Is all of this too trivial for Yom Kippur? I've been intensely writing the Days of Awe so the arrival of the Big Day is almost a relief. It's over, it seems. Without God's judgment?

Yom Kippur without God's judgment feels like running down the football field and, standing on the five-yard line, spiking the ball.

Yom Kippur Serious.

Resisting Yom Kippur.

Going About Your Business Yom Kippur.

Laughing About The Guy Carrying An Umbrella On The Beach Yom Kippur.

You have to keep religious authorities on their toes. So they're always guessing what you'll sign on to and what you won't.

God, too. As I've often thought: "No" to God's judgment without a discussion where argument, even defiance, is allowed. Encouraged.

The power God has. The conscience I have. I'm not made to simply say yes. Should I? We?

Arguing with God is, like the prophetic and exile, indigenous to Jewish life. Homegrown. Wonderfully difficult and crushing. Humbling. Trauma City. Freeing. Strength needed. Gratitude?

Drama for sure. Endless. I can't imagine life without it.

Can the prophetic address God with boldness on Yom Kippur? If it's not written in the Good Book, write it now. But if you look carefully, you'll find the prophetic here and there on Yom Kippur.

Without that bold address to God. And the feeling that the prophetic might happen any moment. And deservedly so. The Torah collapses in on itself.

The Torah as Trigger City.

Can you imagine God without dissent? I can't.

On fasting, my friend and I agree. Coffee in the morning. Breaking the fast in mid-afternoon.

There isn't a Jewish tradition of fasting throughout the year so that it becomes part of our spiritual discipline. And we're not going to repent and change anyway. The injustice we are committing and enabling as a community will continue. So what gives with the fasting?

I did fast until a bit after noon when the Tzedek service, a good one, ended. Though, as with all Yom Kippur services, Tzedek's went past my timeframe.

Still, Zoom makes it possible for me to attend services. Like the ones I attended as a child, with much regret, to be honest. I didn't understand what was going on then. Or why.

I rebelled. Quite properly. Yet through all the junk I experienced in Hebrew school, a seed was planted. It's still in process. There's so much water under the bridge since my childhood. The water keeps flowing. Strong currents.

A real flood it is, without Noah's Ark appearing. I look to the horizon. As I do each morning. I see less and less hope.

Is history a flood without an ark?

Ingrained within my consciousness is Rubenstein's understanding of history as a cycle of violence and atrocity without end. When I heard him speak this so many years ago, I couldn't accept it. Nor could I deny it. Still.

What to do with this except live our lives. As a witness. To?

Rabbi Rosen's sermon was on white privilege and the battle to extend or defeat it. Where do we stand as Jews, he asked. Or rather assumed. For me, as Rabbi Rosen knows, this is a subject for Jews as American citizens, not Jews as Jews.

The central question facing us as Jews is Israel-Palestine. Full stop. Rabbi Rosen spoke about this last night. Must every sermon be about Israel-Palestine?

Rabbi Rosen's sermon was moving in its way but for me the real breakthrough is his reframing of ancient texts and prayers. For Yom Kippur, as it is each year, it is Isaiah 58 with Rabbi Rosen's specific references to modern forms of theft, abuse of power, militarization.

Those who know Rabbi Rosen know the drill. There is power in bringing the old Isaiah, as cutting as he was, into the present.

Also Tzedek's Martyrology. Recited for those who died trying to bring a better life into being. Typical of Tzedek, its martyrology isn't restricted to Jews.

What happens when all your prayer dreams come true? When everything that wasn't prayed about suddenly is. Like some churches on the margins, Tzedek is a dream come true.

Sermons too. Everything you wanted to hear in a sermon and never did. All of a sudden is spoken out loud by the rabbi, for God's sake! Without hiding and without clever hints that still allow for congregational peace.

A new dilemma. Because when all of your dreams come true you want to see them beam down into life. When they don't – when they won't – what to do?

As for the Palestinian – African American dialogue, certainly radical for almost any other Jewish community in America, I found it of some value but was also disappointed. The discussion's grounding, in future realizations of what real justice would mean, limited its impact. We won't be getting anywhere near there.

We live in dystopian times. We need a dystopian solidarity.

The really good stuff, over and over again, won't do.

An example from the dialogue: Is Israel's settler-colonialism as a historical viewpoint translatable politically? Or an important historical viewpoint a politics negotiates?

Another example: What does a boldly declared anti-Zionism rendered historically mean politically in the present?

There's a reason we don't discuss, rather than assume, these viewpoints. Nuance disrupts bold declarations.

This is where the state of loss, itself a mourning, is right now. Its tune, for me at least, is whistling in the dark.

How else to protect ourselves from the notion that the Israeli occupation of Palestine is permanent, than leaving the political ground for a future destined to arrive so late it won't matter or be worth the struggle and its costs.

A few minutes ago, my friend, part of our Jewish future, left for home. We had an important time together. Heart to heart.

Religious services, by Zoom or in person, are for me, formal rather than spiritual occasions. Though spirit can be found in the formal, a certain kind of public affirmation, the limitations are important.

To what end, I wonder, as Yom Kippur shuts down for another year. As if the place we'll find ourselves next year will be so different. Or more or less the same. Maybe a step or two better. Perhaps worse.

Out to the beach crossover for me. After a late afternoon rain.

Tomorrow is ordinary time. Where I, we, the world, returns. Where we left off.

AFTER LIGHT

SEPTEMBER 17

Waking. The Day After. Feeling bereft. Is it that Yom Kippur is over or that my friend has left the scene?

Yom Kippur leave-taking awaits its yearly turn; my friend is back home to his real life.

Arrival and departures. Returns. To be on and, at some point, off the scene, forever. Our days marked. By.

Is life a charade or something akin to all things must pass away?

The musical lines that arrive, unbidden, from decades ago, are small comfort. More comforting than Isaiah 58 though. Especially when I think – we should know? – that Isaiah's second half, the return to God's ways, is his aspirational self.

In a twist, are Isaiah's condemnations the other side of his aspirational self?

Imagine Constantinian Jews hearing Isaiah. On the fast that will not do anything but make things worse. Then celebrating breaking the fast as a huge achievement. Bigger than big. Like Catholics intoning – "Lord I am not worthy" – then standing obediently in line for communion.

What gives all around? The interfaith ecumenical deal is the Big Time.

My God! Our liturgies go on and on. They are endless.

Our consolation?

Is there a breaking point to our ability to survive the dissonance that rises beyond the heavens into some other universe?

Faith as space travel. The heavens are full of God's glory and our confessions and lack thereof.

Written in the Book of Life, as I apparently am.

Is God the only judgment writer in the universe?

Since I am alive this morning, I write. In my own Book of Life.

It's still dark outside. I await my liturgical prompt. To head out for first light.

First light. After light. How beautiful it is this morning.

Seeing first light as I walked toward the beach, I crossed over. Thinking, with the high tide, I wouldn't make it to my Chapel of Love this morning. Then I kept walking.

I arrive to find a hammock with a young man inside sleeping, his backpack and skateboard beneath him. I saw him last year – Hammock Guy I call him. I don't know if he's homeless or just travels around.

There was another young man there too. He snapped some photos and left. I hesitate to think my Chapel of Love is becoming a tourist destination.

The submarine I saw a few days ago is back. Any Jews on board?

I'm out of the Chapel now. With the sun rising and sunrise folks ambling on the beach. Not a crowd exactly yet more people than usual. A sure sign of an impending rocket lunch.

I needed to get to my Chapel of Love this morning and keep walking. Since earth bound I am, let the peaks of the religious calendars, all of them, be suspended for now. See where things go, if anywhere.

What if the Days of Awe just went away for a while? Passover, too. Christmas and Easter. Ramadan. What would the Biblical Isaiah say to this challenge? Rabbi Rosen's Isaiah? Can we experiment with our holy days when injustice goes on all around us?

Can we responsibly get off our collective religious merry-go-round? Can we responsibly keep going on our collective religious merry-go-round?

Our religious calendars are moving targets – that don't go anywhere. What is our still point? Is there a still point in history?

If there is still point in history, it may be utopian. It may be dystopian.

The Days of Awe have their own history. The Traveling Arks, Torahs inside, that accompany Israel's soldiers. The Holocaust Arks, makeshift, in the death camps. Jews tortured with German orders. Now the reversal; Hebrew infected with atrocity.

I walk, trying to unscramble the scrambled.

Home now. As I came closer to home, surfers arrived. The sky darkened. What appeared to be a morning of expanding light, dimmed. Both phases held their beauty high, though.

Different light. Find what you will.

I wonder if my sons will find their way in life.

Did I?

First light. After light.

Is the time after light arrives and leaves what belief in the afterlife is all about?

Afterlight. What remains. Of.

Prophet afterlife. Isaiah 58 cut us to the core still.

Late light. The light we realize came and went. Yet remains.

Bible light. Flickering. When it's strong. When it's weak. Full blast is too much.

Biblical Isaiah isn't a lesson to be learned, memorized, stalked.

Biblical Isaiah is a haunting reminder. Of.

Prophet light. What to do with what won't come true?

The truth that does or doesn't set us free.

Late afternoon, with rain. Heading toward Shabbat. Our religious calendar moves on.

I plan to Zoom Tzedek's half-hour candle lighting gathering tonight and if there is a Torah study, Saturday morning, I'll be there too.

I'm becoming a regular Torah study attendee it seems. I even advised one of my Facebook friends that he could receive regular information on the goings on at Tzedek by joining the synagogue. He isn't Jewish. It doesn't matter; all are welcome.

I wonder what is becoming of me. Is the rebellious Jew. In old age. Playing it safe?

I am not a Diaspora Jew for sure. I am not a Rabbinic Jew either. Tzedek features both parts. I dip in for what I want. I do learn from a trained rabbi. With a conscience. Why not?

Being a simple Jew from North Miami Beach, Florida, I had to speak when others were silent. Now others are speaking.

I listen and pick up the pieces I missed, didn't know or rebelled against learning.

We never know when tides – and winds – will change. It has happened in some Jewish places. While I'm still here. I didn't expect it. Wow!

Speaking of which, Rabbi Rosen's first sermon of Yom Kippur, which I missed, has arrived in text. It is strong as I heard. And, declining the periphery, Rabbi Rosen moves right to the center – Israel-Palestine. He doesn't go soft at the center. Not at all.

Rabbi Rosen forgoes consolation, openness and building bridges. Just the opposite. He quotes from the recent Israeli human rights document that announces Israel as creating and practicing an apartheid system. He calls out the progressive solution of dealing with division within the Jewish community, the so-called Open Tent approach. Open for what and for whom, he asks.

The political, indeed ethical and spiritual situation is too grave for mere acceptance of dissent. For the supposedly greater value of having dissenters feel included in the mainstream Jewish community. According to Rabbi Rosen, the Open Tent concept is a deflection. It delays the judgment Yom Kippur calls for.

Inclusion in injustice cannot be the watchword for Jews.

There's something more. Rabbi Rosen announced a new ambition – opened up by his principles and by Zoom. To build a "Global Congregation of Conscience." Interestingly, he doesn't say for Jews only, if that isn't ambitious enough. Tzedek is for anyone of conscience who finds Tzedek's way the way for them.

So many people have been waiting for Jewish to stand up. Rabbi Rosen seems to be saying: "Here it is."

Yom Kippur is behind us. Shabbat is on the horizon.

I remember my years of isolation and abandonment. The threats against me that arrived by mail and phone. During my speaking engagements. In hotels I slept in. From many quarters, including from rabbis and other Jewish establishment types. How I was smeared and pursued and investigated. The trauma inflicted. The backs turned of those who "support" me. The solidarity that wasn't. Still, mostly, isn't.

Oh well. I have my integrity intact. And a take on authority from the right, the center and the Left, which is cautionary. To say the least.

When you're labeled the worst or the best, a turncoat or a prophet, you are on your own.

SEPTEMBER 18

Shabbat. Waking too early. The day after, after.

The Days of Awe don't pass quickly. Even when they're over. If you're not a Constantinian Jew, that is. Or a fellow traveler. With the perks of Constantinianism. Of all faiths.

On the other side of the Jewish ledger – the Days of Awe aftertaste. Can Jews of Conscience help in the building of a Global Congregation of Conscience. Is such a mission hubris?

Think small. Then smaller. That's where I've landed.

Yesterday on the news, if I heard right. Are there 10,000 plus Haitians, under a bridge, in a Texas border town, to be deported, one by one?

Isaiah 58 looms large. Our fasting. To what end?

I Zoomed Tzedek's Shabbat candle lighting last night but, once again, I wasn't prepared with my candles and wine. Where to find challah in my beloved Cape?

There's a limit to Zoom's reach into our interior lives, I think.

Are our interior lives growing or shrinking? Perhaps they're mostly the same through time. Only time will tell.

I remember church services held under a Texas bridge where I lived a decade ago. The intentions were real, yet I wondered what it was like for those who had homes to return home after the services. While those without homes remained on the streets.

Is prayer enough to comfort the wealthy and the homeless at the very same moment – if God is listening in?

Perhaps the idea was uplift. If you get right with Jesus, a home will appear.

Yes, I don't think Global This or Global That will do much except dig a deeper hole. I don't think celebrating indigenous peoples are the way out of this mess either.

So many illusions. We all have them. The Days of Awe may contribute to the illusion pile that grows around us. Though we continue to hope for a breakthrough every year.

Maybe Yom Kippur is the Jewish twin to the Christian Second Coming wish list.

If Jews truly turn. Toward. Or Jesus returned. Here. I doubt anyone would know what to do with themselves.

In my Chapel of Love. First light is a wonderful blue sky with a band of orange on the horizon. Pink highlights in the middle of the sky. Birds are flying. High tide, so uneven footing, but the tide is beginning to lower for my walk back home.

Now back out on the beach, the sun rising. Pretty.

Thinking as I walk home about how many times I've made this journey. Same time. Same place. Not bored. Always something new.

Late-style Life. When everything falls apart. And lands in its place. Unknown before. I'm not done journeying with Edward Said who wrote of Late-style and who also fell and landed in his unknown before place.

Late-style Days of Awe.

Late-style Yom Kippur.

Can the Late-style Prophetic carry both. As they fall in in their unknown place?

The prophet carries the world as it falls.

Home. After breakfast, Tzedek's Torah study. My last of the Days of Awe round-up. Up for study – Deuteronomy 32. Another barnburner.

What a God we Jews have! Easy to take potshots at God's temper tantrums, petty jealousies and more. Easier to smooth things out.

I certainly agree with cutting the hard edges. Yet it's also true, as I raised in the discussion this morning, that without this difficult God, the prophetic is impossible. Our ability to speak for justice and even to say to God – "Enough with the bellowing!" – comes from this overbearing presence.

That some years ago a French Jew called "the Jewish prison."

True enough, though, we need a distance from many of these canonical texts and divine attributes. Selective we have to be. Yet that's true with every tradition. And the history that's created by its followers.

When I think of God's wake in the Torah, I think of Christian and Islamic history. Of other religions. Of Modernity. To which every knee bends. One way or another.

With our parsed God, is the prophetic walking through borrowed time?

There's a difference between those who had to struggle with the too strong God and those who inherit God's displacement. Indeed, even among theologians there's less and less discussion about God.

Rebellion achieved has its own questions and limitations.

Yes, it was through one of my encounters with Said that I had to face that question once and for all.

Said was ill, already facing death, when I received an invitation to deliver a paper at a conference in his honor – with Said in attendance. I chose to present on Said's understanding of exile, as he experienced it, which he wrote of in several essays.

At that time, I was writing of my own experience of exile. Said's exile was, at least in the beginning, geographic, his family's leave-taking of Palestine. My exile came later and was communal, my distance from a newly militarized Jewish community.

Said made it abundantly clear that his exile had no religious connotation – as far as I know, Said rarely, if ever, contemplated the possibility of God. For years, through Holocaust theology, I had held God at a distance with questions that God provided no answers for: Where was God in the Holocaust?

Yet as I contemplated what later became a book, *Practicing Exile*, I had to ask the question of God in a different way. Not where was God in history, a real question to be sure, but whether I could survive my deepening exile without God.

I sat on a cushion each morning as a form of meditation, clearing my head, beginning again. I began by posing the question to God. For which, predictably, I received no answer. Then I reversed the process and posed the question to myself.

Instead of focusing on the Grand Design, the universe. Or the particular question of peoplehood, the Jewish universe, I downsized. I asked myself – on a personal level, for me on my journey – if I could make it much further without God.

Instead of an answer, I felt a response arrive deep within me.

My response: In my deepening exile, and unlike Said, I could not make it without God.

When I made the decision, hearing and feeling my response, that as a Jew, I could not make it in exile without God, I did not – I knew I could not – make a claim beyond my person.

I don't know if, objectively speaking, there is a God. Hanging out in heaven. Or present here on earth.

That Big Box God remains an open question. I certainly would never make a public claim about a God of History. That Other Big Box God, remains an open question, too.

I find it better, healthier, and more realistic to forgo answers to those questions. The answers of which are unavailable to us.

Our understandings of God are constructions and our deconstructions of God are constructions, too. Almost all theology today, maybe all of it, from Black theology to feminist theology, represent deconstructions and reconstructions of God. These efforts are about us and how the naming of God functions in society and our psyche.

I follow these discussions with interest, at least in the past I did; they have little or no impact on my decision. That I could not be in exile, as a Jew, without God.

In the end, it's really that simple: As a Jew I accept that God chose us from among the nations, and that our calling is special. In the morning I thank God for making me a Jew and calling me to be free. When I don't say my prayer, when I don't feel like it for different reasons, I am quite aware of what I am not saying. I am affirming what that morning I am silent about.

Thanking God for making me a Jew and calling me to be free is part of the prayer I created for my children. From their early days, we would say the prayer together in the morning before they left for school. I thought I created the prayer for them. I think now it was a preliminary step, preparation for my continuing journey.

How else to practice exile as a Jew. At the end of ethical Jewish history?

For exile, as Said thought, is a practice rather than a belief. Practicing exile is a grounding in tradition, in the present, in history, as an individual. The challenge of God, rather than knowledge of God, is part of the grounding in the questions and accompaniment that allows us to draw near, to embrace and to embody the prophetic, the Jewish indigenous.

What more there is to being a Jew is commentary. Let the discussion continue.

Practicing exile at the end of ethical Jewish history is uncharted terrain. Perhaps it is the reversal of Deuteronomy, the last book of the Torah.

Practicing exile isn't an exaltation or an exhortation. Nothing is going to be conquered or vanquished.

At the end of ethical Jewish history, practicing exile is keeping head above water, dealing with trauma that won't heal, while continuing to be open to the possibility of gratitude. For life as it has been given to and chosen by us.

The prophet, deeply aware of Jewish history,
looks to the right and to the left and goes his own way.

PART TWO

Meditations on the Late-Style Jewish Prophetic in the New Diaspora

Encountering the prophetic voice is to feel its force, its ancient cadence, its contemporary relevance.

PRACTICING EXILE

WHAT JEWS CARRY with them into exile will help determine the future of Jewish identity and commitment. What does it mean to be faithful as a Jew?

The struggle to be faithful as a Jew has always had its share of difficulty, even, and sometimes especially, within the folds of the broader Jewish community. External pressures have always been present. Internal struggles, too. Jews of Conscience face a series of challenges, some of them old hand, others in a new key. Varying external and internal forces remain.

Since Jews of Conscience are small in number what happens to them individually and as a collective may seem of little importance to the broader global currents where the great majority of the world lives and breathes. Yet as carriers of the global root of the prophetic, Jews of Conscience are important beyond their numbers. In some ways, the fate of the global prophetic is enhanced or diminished by Jews of Conscience who draw near, embrace and embody the indigenous Jewish prophetic.

How Jews of Conscience practice Jewishness in their exile can enhance or diminish others who are in exile from their own communities, nations and religions. For, as is often the case, the Jewish condition helps illumine the condition of others. In our time there is a globalization of exile and, within this globalization, exiles from one community interact with exiles of other communities. The interaction of exiles portends a sharing of experience, both negative and positive. Though the Jewish experience of exile is illustrative of a broader shared experience, the sharing of exile perspectives portends a mutuality in the making.

Practicing exile together is more than sharing faith experiences and listening to the discourse of others often defined as the interfaith dialogue. The practice of exile portends an interfaith solidarity that arrives within a new context. That context is less about the communication of the greatness of our traditions in their fullness and more about gathering the fragments of traditions that have been abused and squandered. The practice of exile across traditions is about realizing that each community configuration has reached some kind of end point. Our sharing of exile is defined mostly by sharing what is left.

Jews are a test case of sharing what is left, since the Jewish tradition is long and has been tried by rhetorical and literal fire. As the broader Jewish community is newly empowered and thus culpable in the ways of the world, Jews of Conscience are abandoning normative Jewish life without the prospect of return. There is permanence to Jewish exile and, in that permanence, a singular challenge to the future of Jewish particularity. Part of this challenge is a question of numbers, but a larger challenge has to do with Christianity, Islam and some of the broader currents of modernity. In all three, Jews are singled out for praise and derision.

In much of the world avoiding Jews, or rather Jewish, is difficult, whether living Jews are present physically or not. "The Jew" is almost everywhere in the world, even though Jews are mostly concentrated in Israel and America. Jews in the Gospels and the Quran take a central place in the Christian and Islamic canon and mythology. That place is neither all good nor all bad. Rather, both Christianity and Islam are ambivalent about Jews, an ambivalence that pervades the broader currents of modern and global culture.

Part of this ambivalence goes back to the instability found at the heart of Jewish history and belief. From the beginning, the people Israel and Israel's God have featured instability as the fate of both and the key to another kind of stability characterized by the refusal of idolatry and justice as the pathway to God. In some ways, Christianity and Islam are built upon a closing down of this in/stability through a final messiah and a final prophet. Yet insofar as both Christianity and Islam carry the Jewish seeds of instability in their canonical texts, as previews, Jewish is at their center. Among Christians and Muslims of Conscience today, this finality is being questioned, if not theologically in all cases, at least in the practice of exile. What does it mean to be a Christian or a Muslim in exile without hope of return?

The Jewish experience is not defining of the experience of others in exile. Nonetheless, it is instructive. Jews of Conscience will not define Jewishness in the normative definition of Jews either in the Jewish community or within Christian and Islamic discourses about Jews. In the Jewish community, Constantinian and Progressive Jews will continue to be considered 'authentic' Jews. As well, the Gospels and the Quran will continue to liturgically define Jews in the broader Christian and Islamic world.

The ambivalence about Jews, already embedded in Christianity and Islam for better and for worse, continues unabated. Christians and Muslims of Conscience, though, will ultimately suffer the same fate as Jews in the broader Jewish community; they will be seen as abandoning their tradition and community and may suffer the similar definition of being self-hating Christians and Muslims. Because of the much greater numbers of Christians and Muslims, though, the rebellion of Christians and Muslims of Conscience may be sluffed off or highlighted for various reasons. However, by joining Jews of Conscience in the practice of exile, the ambivalence that Jews experience may signal the same fate for Christians and Muslims of Conscience.

It remains to be seen whether the ambivalence toward Jews in other traditions, even when in exile together, will transfer in whole or in part. The evidence so far is sketchy. Most likely, Jews will come into solidarity with others in exile – and remain set apart. The historic ambivalence toward Jews is too deep to be overcome completely. And for the Jewish part, the disappearance of ambivalence toward Jews of Conscience in exile may not be wanted or accepted completely.

Some of this ambivalence dynamic may be conscious, other parts not. For Jews of Conscience, the question of acceptance and mutuality is shadowed by the part of Jewish particularity from which the prophetic is formed and embodied.

Ambivalence about Jews is not about eternal anti-Semitism or the Jew-hatred that led to the death camps. Rather the ambivalence is more subtle, ingrained in the scriptures of Christianity and Islam, an ambivalence that has existed since the origins of Christianity and Islam. A similar ambivalence exists within the foundational texts of the Enlightenment and is now embedded in the global movement of secular culture.

Jews, as well, have ambivalence about Jewish identity. Like other minorities and persecuted groups, ambivalence toward a community comes from inside as well from outside forces. Internalized ambivalence about identity, even an identity that is prized, often carries a foundational ambivalence. How that ambivalence is worked with and through over time, within the individual and the community, is what matters. How ambivalence functions within the indigenous Jewish prophetic is itself of great interest, especially when it is obvious that the prophetic often leads into a no-person land of critique and suffering.

Regardless of how ambivalence toward Jews and Jewishness, by others and by Jews themselves, proceeds – the contemporary debate about Jewish influence in the media and global economics for example – demonstrates the continuing showcasing of Jews in the twenty-first century. The international discussion of Israel is another case in point. Even the often quite critical but respectful discussion of Israel within Jewish-Palestinian solidarity circles cannot avoid this ambivalence entanglement at times. Simply because Jewish and Palestinian participants are enlightened on these issues does not mean that centuries of religion and culture disappear overnight. Rather, ambivalence has to be negotiated, perhaps like the prophetic itself.

What are the details of the practice of exile? In the Jewish case, the details may involve different stances toward the Jewish tradition, its sacred texts and contemporary belief structures. It may also be the refusal to take on any of parts of the tradition, at least overtly. Yet what appears to be a turning of the back to tradition may ultimately be its embrace. Such is the indigenous quality of the Jewish prophetic, a return as it were to the struggle against idolatry and assimilation.

Some within the Jewish fold and outside of it may wonder if refusal is enough to qualify for the practice of exile. Being on the edges of tradition and society is a long held Jewish position and now, in its new iteration, within the empowered Jewish world. Opposing Jewish empowerment in its present form begs the question if there is an alternative path for Jewish empowerment. More realistically, since there may not be another empowerment path, the Jewish practice of exile for the foreseeable future may simply be a pieced together opposition with whatever in Jewish history and modern culture is at hand. This often involves fragments of other cultural and religious traditions that allow Jews to roam free in traditionally banned foreign precincts. The question remains how far Jews can roam without themselves being called to account. After all, the indigenous prophetic has its limits.

Are Jews who practice exile marking time? Since Jews of Conscience won't ultimately find their way outside Jewish and won't return to Jewish as defined today, the future seems limited. Meanwhile, Jews practicing exile can be found almost everywhere. Perhaps, the indigenous Jewish prophetic, quite alive in our time, without a future, is already at home.

The New Diaspora, named and unnamed, is the future already arrived.

EDWARD SAID AND THE LATE-STYLE JEWISH PROPHETIC

WITH THE RETURN OF JEWS to the historical grid after the Holocaust and the squandering of their prophetic witness in the permanent occupation of Palestine and Palestinians, the root of the prophetic is challenged to the core. Miracle of miracles, or perhaps to be anticipated, at this moment of crises, and against the grain of contemporary Jewish life with its idolatry of Jewish state power, the Jewish prophetic is reborn. On its last legs, battered by the history of suffering and abuse of power, today the Jewish prophetic is undergoing a resurrection of sorts, in the earthly sense, as a struggle for Jewish history, in light of Palestinian suffering and on behalf of those who suffer everywhere.

A Jewish theology of liberation cannot begin today as it once did with the Holocaust or the birth of the state of Israel, as a dynamic of innocence and redemption. Nor can mourning and confession be the primary vehicle for choosing another direction in Israel-Palestine. The colonial and imperial histories of others against Jews can be factored in but only with the colonial and imperial history of Israel highlighted as well. The prophetic, too, must be seen contextually, in a new light, as an evolving call to Jews and those in solidarity with Jews, as the essence of what it means to be Jewish, and in the global context of resistance – at the end of ethical Jewish history.

In this context the first two chapters of my *Toward a Jewish Theology of Liberation*, originally published in 1987, have to be rethought and expanded. "A Shattered Witness," which features the work of Holocaust theologians Richard Rubenstein, Elie Wiesel, Emil Fackenheim and Irving Greenberg, and "The Cost of Jewish Empowerment," which traces the movement of the Jewish community to a neo-conservative political stance as a way of protecting and projecting Israel's power over against Palestinians, needs new content that upends the book's projected optimism. Instead of beginning with the Holocaust, for example, "A Shattered Witness" has to be revised in light of the permanence of Israel's occupation. In sum, Israel, with the enabling assistance of Jews around the world, has shattered the Jewish witness, a second shattering now shared with the Holocaust. "The Cost of Empowerment" has to be refocused on its significance for Jews of Conscience of the end of ethical Jewish history.

Here Edward Said's understanding of "late style," applied to artists of varied kinds by Theodor Adorno and, thinly disguised, indicative of Said's own work at the end of his life, especially as it related to Palestine, is of interest. Though we usually think of late style as the culmination of an artist's life's work, adding another layer to what already has gone before, the crowning achievement as it were, Said via Adorno is more interested in those whose late style involves "nonharmonious, nonserene tension, and above all, a sort of deliberately unproductive productiveness going against." For Said, late style combines "intransigence, difficulty, and unresolved contradiction."

Citing the playwright Henrik Ibsen as an example, Said interprets Ibsen's last work as coming from an "angry and disturbed artist for whom the medium of drama provides an occasion to stir up more anxiety, tamper irrevocably with the possibility of closure, and leave the audience more perplexed and unsettled than before." Said quotes Adorno on the objective/subjective sense of lateness: "Objective is the fractured landscape, subjective the light in which – alone – it glows in life. The artist does not bring about their harmonious synthesis. As the power of dissociation, the artist tears them apart in time, in order perhaps, to preserve them for the eternal. In the history of art, late works are the catastrophes." Interpreting Adorno, Said writes that "lateness is the idea of surviving beyond what is acceptable and normal; in addition, lateness includes the idea that one cannot really go beyond lateness at all, cannot transcend or lift oneself out of lateness, but can only deepen the lateness."

At the end of ethical Jewish history, the prophetic has entered its own late style, what I call the "Late-Style Jewish

Prophetic." Such a prophetic moment, assertive and on the ropes, comes from an ancient tradition while being performed anarchically in the present, and is permanently exiled without a conscious desire to return. The Late-Style Jewish Prophetic has a sometimes interest in God, though for the most part seeks a considered yet mostly unarticulated distance from God, as it throws its lot in with the dispossessed of all stripes, while believing its Jewishness is a given that needs little exploration or definition.

At the end of ethical Jewish history, the Late-Style Jewish Prophetic struggles against the final assimilation it knows intuitively to be the enablement of and silence about injustice. Rejecting the coloniality and imperialism within the Jewish prophetic itself, the Late-Style Jewish Prophetic stops at the boundary line of the Promised Land, as if its decision to say "no" to the oppression of Palestinians now somehow redresses ancient Israel's original violent entry into the land.

Most of this definitional detail, even the conceptual framework itself, is embodied in the Late-Style Jewish Prophetic without an overt embrace of Jewish history or the history of the prophetic's back story. Rather, it is buried in the deep subconscious of the ancient and indigenous prophetic which, in its late style, explodes in our time. Irony of ironies, or perhaps fittingly, the Jewish prophetic, which for centuries turned itself outward to the non-Jewish world, has returned to its original internal Jewish witness revolving around the Promised Land, Israel-Palestine. Arriving home, the Late-Style Jewish Prophetic finds that the Jewish community, the majority of whom dwell securely within the empire formations of Israel, America, and Europe, have departed, on the justice question, for parts unknown. Or perhaps better understood, the ancient Empire Divide of choosing community or empire, a divide where Jews have dwelled and fought over Jewish destiny from time immemorial, has widened to such an extent that any bridge back is a bridge too far.

What happens when a bridge back is a bridge too far? Where do those searching for a bridge go? The old disciplines are inadequate; the new ones are developing in real-time. The Late-Style Jewish Prophetic, already arrived, needs sourcing and exploration.

Is the task ahead to be defined as fill-in-the-blanks as the Late-Style Jewish Prophetic unfolds? If so, the narration of its meaning and content is after the prophetic's arrival. And since the prophetic is still moving, the narration has to be in real-time. The dynamic, though, hasn't been and probably won't be linear, a protest no doubt of the tradition as handed down in a linear way. Thus, the Late-Style Jewish Prophetic, in its deconstruction, will no doubt fight its narration. As if, what appeared in revolt will now assume a normative structure. It is against this very structure that the Late-Style Jewish Prophetic protests.

Perhaps the Late-Style Jewish Prophetic is anarchistic by its very nature in a similar way that the Biblical prophets were before they were remembered and thus drawn by the editors, redactors and interpreters of the Biblical text. The difference is that the

Biblical prophets became, if they didn't begin, as composite figures; those who embody the Late-Style Jewish Prophetic are real beings that resist this process. Yet it may be important to start locating their witness, for their own sake and for the future, if not for the Jewish world, then for others of different traditions who are entering their own late-style prophetic. This could be the truest and most important universalization of the Jewish prophetic appropriate for our time.

As much as its anarchistic sensibility, of interest here is how the Late-Style Jewish Prophetic is linked with tradition in its embodiment of a dystopic solidarity. Speaking directly to the Jewish community as its first act, with a calling to return to justice, and with the Jewish community's rejection of its plea, the prophetic in its late style has moved in another direction. With no return in sight, the desire for return has also waned. Whereas the Biblical prophets often called upon Israel's enemies to discipline Israel's waywardness, the Late-Style Jewish Prophetic, chastened by Jewish suffering in the Holocaust and its abuse of power toward Palestinians, has entered an uncharted terrain. Jews of Conscience cannot call on Israel's enemies to discipline Israel's waywardness and that waywardness, while it might one day lessen, has already crossed the line of no return. Even if history catches up with Israel's abuse of power, it will be too late; the Jewish tradition and now its history is been infected with atrocity. Whatever innocence there was within Jewish, a defining point for modern Jewry, there will be no return to innocence.

This "no return" is what separates Progressive Jews from Jews of Conscience.

What is the prophetic without the possibility of return? In fact, return in the Jewish tradition is, when justice is aborted, the only pathway to God. Whether the actual history that the Biblical prophets experienced featured such a return is in question; in our actual history Jews of Conscience know this is unlikely to happen. At least, Jews of Conscience should know that, if it happens, it will not occur in their lifetime. Rhetorically, some Jews of Conscience, project this occurrence in the "world to come." Yet, one doubts their ability to truly believe this scenario.

Can the world to come coalesce with the breakdown the Late-Style Jewish Prophetic is undergoing? It may be that another possibility of the world is represented by Jews of Conscience simply be embodying, in its deconstruction, the prophetic itself. Since there seems to be no way forward, the only viable path may be continuation in the only way possible.

Instability is the prophet's wake. Is this because the God that originally called the prophets is unstable?

NOTES ON THE LATE-STYLE JEWISH PROPHETIC

THINKING OF DETAILS, contours, borders and boundaries of Jewish history, the prophets, Jewish. Can I think what has arrived but hasn't, as yet, become articulate? Writing what has arrived has a long history in many traditions and movements. Often that arrival is disputed by those who cannot abide what is – what has come into being. Often, too, those who carry that arrival, those who embody it, only glimpse what they represent.

Thus, the misunderstanding of misunderstandings occurs. Of why those who oppose the arrival oppose who embody it. Since, at least on the surface, everything seems so clear to those Jews who can no longer abide by the boundaries and borders drawn by the normative Jewish community.

Unpacking the Late-Style Jewish Prophetic is hardly simple or definitive. Much needs to be uncovered and discovered. Here are some elements that I can think of at this moment. Without imposing any particular order:

~ 1 ~

In the Late-Style Jewish Prophetic, the prophetic is seen less as a tradition one is beholden to or even a tradition one is in continuity with, though elements of tradition and continuity are obvious. Contemporary Jews who embody the prophetic are sometimes knowledgeable about the Jewish tradition but most often are less than expert in it. Studying the tradition of the Jewish prophetic can be helpful, usually as a way of becoming more articulate about what the person already possesses. In fact, the contemporary Jewish prophets are, almost to the person, what Said calls "intransigent amateurs" who attempt to gather light in the darkness. By and large, experts on the Jewish tradition, whether leaders of Jewish organizations, academics or rabbis, are lost in the injustice of Israel and have enabled this injustice, indeed worked overtime to censor dissent, especially of those who speak with a prophetic voice.

~ 2 ~

As light gatherers, the Jewish prophets today are identifiable to Jews and others and, in another sense, a mystery. How in fact are they Jewish? In whose name do they speak and act? What claims do they make for their calling, if any? Has God sent them or do they appear as if they have arrived from Somewhere Else? According to the Jewish tradition, the era of the Jewish prophets ended thousands of years ago. Called by God in the Promised Land, condemning the injustice done within and by the Chosen People and sometimes with the strangers counted among them, the prophets call on Israel to return to justice and thus God, all within the context of an articulated destiny among the nations. Now Jews have returned to the land after so much history and pain to find many Jews who are terribly disenchanted, some of whom ultimately leave Israel in light of conscience, thus seemingly contradicting the Jewish Biblical view of the promise itself. Are these Jews, donning the prophetic mantle, in conflict with parts of the Biblical promise and prophetic tradition itself?

~ 3 ~

The Late-Style Jewish Prophetic arrives at the end of ethical Jewish history; it does not seek the destruction of the Jewish tradition or its elevation. Even if once embraced, renewal and return are now the farthest things from its agenda. The injustice toward Palestinians, now permanent, is too much. The Jewish prophetic voice is therefore isolated, in exile and without redress. Though Jews of Conscience grow in number, lateness is its sensibility; pining for victory means cutting its sails, turning away from the truth of what is obvious. Jewish ethical values built up through tradition and a long history of suffering and struggle have been squandered.

~ 4 ~

Leaning on the tradition in the form of recovering rabbinic religiosity or appropriating New Age sensibilities won't do. The state of Israel continues apace. Dissent loses the day. Jews live within a Jewish state and outside it but the sense of homecoming, exile and the diaspora as it has been known, is over. Whether living in Israel, leaving Israel for other parts of the globe, living in America or Argentina, the Jewish Diaspora is no more. How can there be a diaspora with the state established and Jews, either refusing to reside there or Israelis leaving the state? If Israel is a homecoming that has been squandered, and with a state Jews can, if they want, return to, how to explain the increasing dissent even over Israel's claim to be a Jewish state? From now on, the Jewish population of Israel will only experience natural increase and attrition. The dynamic of exile and return, so central to the Jewish understanding of history, continues to recede.

~ 5 ~

The presence of the God of Israel, battered by the history of Jewish suffering and the Holocaust, is further diminished by Israel's unjust policies toward Palestinians. The Jewish prophets of today, whatever their personal spirituality, rarely claim the Jewish tradition or the Jewish God of History as their guide. Despite this, the prophetic remains possible because once given in history, the prophetic, like the covenant, has assumed an independent existence. Neither the prophetic nor the covenant is any longer dependent on God. Yet, at the same time, it seems difficult to understand the prophetic as self-generating. The prophetic, which endangers the security and the safety of those who embody it and, most often, in a losing effort, must have a foundational source outside the individual. This source, often unnamed – unnamable? – might be described as coming from Somewhere Else. Somewhere Else is less about mysticism and more about a traveling entity which entered and continues in history with the power to survive those within and outside Jewish history who attempt to explain away, discipline or destroy it.

~ 6 ~

The prophetic, ancient and late, is distinctive to the Jewish tradition. At the same time, it is the root of the global prophetic. As with all traditions, the Jewish prophetic has elements within it that need disciplining. Parts of the prophetic tradition are worthy of renewed consideration, the emphasis on justice being the most obvious, while others parts, God-sanctioned violence comes to mind, must be jettisoned altogether. Elements of the Jewish prophetic tradition now exist in other traditions, even though they have often been expropriated and used, in turn, to denigrate the Jewish tradition and Jews themselves. Regardless, through their own discernment, through their late style prophetic, other traditions have embraced the Jewish prophetic. For example, Christian liberation theologies have emerged over the last decades – variations of Black, Womanist, Feminist, Latin American, African and Asian, Indigenous and Queer theologies of liberation. Though many of the communities which have developed these theologies were "conquered by the Gospels" and historically embraced a colonial and imperial religion as their own, the prophetic has turned the "historical gospels" they suffered – for example the Gospel of 1492, the Gospel of Colonialism, the Gospel of the Slave Trade and the Gospel of Treblinka – into a resistance that has reshaped the global perspective on the prophetic. In our day and age, through support for Palestinians, these various prophetic movements re-present the prophetic, the Jewish indigenous, to Jews in Israel and outside of it. This embrace and re-presentation of the Jewish prophetic encompass the most radical religious and political revolution of our time.

~ 7 ~

There is only one reason today to be Jewish; to draw near, to embrace and to embody the prophetic. All the rest is commentary. Everything in Jewish history revolves around the prophetic; all Jewish roads lead to the embracing and/or deflecting of the prophetic. Almost every episode in the Hebrew Bible should be seen through this prophetic lens. Ancient Israel and its heirs tell us clearly: Without the prophetic there is no meaning in history or our lives; there may be no meaning in history or our lives;

the prophet embodies the possibility of meaning in history and our lives. This is true about God as well; rather than certainty or negation, the prophet embodies the possibility of God. Thus the Jewish prophetic shifts the religious gamble from belief in and the sovereignty of God. Rather, the prophetic is the embodied gamble that, in the end, there is meaning in history and our lives. The way of assessing the stakes inherent in such a gamble is by embodying the prophetic. All of this with the sure knowledge that the prophetic is destined to fail. Fidelity within the context of the prophetic, even and especially in its failure, is the essence of the meaning in history and our lives. If there is such a meaning.

~ 8 ~

The continuing failure of the prophetic and now, in its late style, the refusal of the prophetic to seek renewal or return; the willingness of the prophetic to discern the colonial and imperial aspects of its own inheritance and listen to those who, in solidarity with Jewish history, re-present the Jewish prophetic to the Jewish world which has squandered its own indigenous, all of this testifies to the resilience and strength of the Jewish prophetic. What will happen with the Jewish prophetic and Jews in general over the long run is not the primary or even secondary concern of the prophetic. For the foreseeable future the defining question for those who embody the Jewish prophetic – the

The renewal of Jewish Diaspora religiosity, so common today, is a deflection from the central issue of the right of Palestinians to be free in their own homeland.

ability of Palestinians to be free in their own homeland. Other issues, even if important in their own right, are a deflection. The issue of Palestinians is the issue that Jews should and must stand up for as Jews. Other issues of justice, for example immigration and BlackLivesMatter in America, should be addressed by Jews as American citizens. At this point, there is little reason to identify as Jews in these arenas since the universal aspect of justice is for all wherever we live. Yet this means that the Palestinian issue of freedom in their homeland is a terminus issue for the Jewish prophetic. In the Late-Style Jewish Prophetic there is nothing less or more before it. Whether there is anything after justice is finally achieved or ultimately denied is a question for the future.

~ 9 ~

The abuse of Jewish power over Palestine and Palestinians and the re-presentation by non-Jews of the Jewish prophetic to the Jewish community which has squandered it, hardly means that Jews are accepted in the post-Holocaust world in and for themselves. That attitudes toward Jews have shifted in a substantially positive direction in much of the world is without question. Yet too many people and communities, including many progressive political and religious activists, still hold ambivalent views about Jews. Despite the clarion call for an intersectional politics, and in light of the regressive attitudes in different parts of the world, Jews are still viewed in complicated ways. Individual Jews in power as well as collective Jewish empowerment are often viewed with suspicion, as tribal, aggressive and out for wealth and power only. The conspiracy list is long. Ancient stereotypes about Jews remain in elite and street culture, emerging at times of crisis and struggle. Israel's behavior and the use of Jewish empowerment in America to discipline dissent about Israel have upped this tension considerably. Anyone, Jew or non-Jew, who speaks publicly on the issues of the Holocaust and Israel-Palestine knows this "ambivalence" terrain well.

~ 10 ~

Without some kind of empowerment, Jews are vulnerable. The notion that Jews are treated as any other group or that, in a pinch, others will come to the aid of Jews is possible, yet far from assured. The acceptance of Jews as Jews, with a defined sense of particularity, remains problematic. The Jewish Question remains. With all the negative discussion about Jewish power, some of it appropriate, some of it with echoes of anti-Semitism, it needs to be said: The idea of Jewish empowerment in a state is not, in and of itself, wrong. That this empowerment permanently oppresses another people is, in and of itself, wrong. That Israel is a colonial state and therefore has no right to exist ignores the history of anti-Semitism and even the diversity found within the early Zionist movement and Israel itself today. The idea increasingly put forth by many that it would be best for Jews and

Palestinians to dwell together in one democratic secular state is an ideal one can support in good faith. Still, it might have been better for Jews and Palestinians to begin their solidarity in two states, two real states. That Israel, with their Jewish and Christian enablers, foreclosed that possibility, is a crime against the Palestinian people. As well, it is a crime against Jewish history. Dwelling and responding to history and the historical context, the Late-Style Jewish Prophetic is engaged with the injustice of Israel with regard to the Palestinian people. The insistence of justice for Palestinians remains. Nonetheless, the prophetic in all its phases, while arguing in no uncertain terms, has always understood that there is a difference between the ideals of justice and the lives of ordinary people in social and political systems. That is, the prophetic has always entered into a level of negotiation to find a way forward. The prophetic is always negotiated.

~11~

Jews are no longer a diaspora people. Thus Diaspora Judaism, with the spiritual formation of Rabbinic Judaism, is over. Today, the overwhelming majority of Jews reside in the American and Israeli empires and with the remnants of European Jewry factored in, including the augmented Russian presence in Israel, the percentages are even higher. Even Jewish dissenters, though marginalized and pursued by Constantinian Jews, or in another way of naming them, Empire Jews, are protected by empire.

The Jewish Diaspora as known through history is thus over because of the overwhelming empowerment and inclusion of an extremely high percentage of Jews worldwide, a *novum* in Jewish history, and because Jews dominate Israel and can move freely in the United States and Europe. As well, the possibility of return to Israel as Jews who live in the traditional diaspora has been consistently and definitely rejected by Jews who continue to live outside Israel. This, as a significant percentage of Israeli Jews continue to emigrate from Israel to different parts of the globe, thus engaging, whether spoken or not, the traditional diaspora, albeit with a twist, as the Promised Land. With this concentration of Jews outside Israel it is important to note that there are still significant parts of the world, including in Europe, where Jews, in significant numbers, remain unwelcome. This places the Jewish prophetic in a new context from which it lives and journeys. Like Israel's occupation of Palestine and Palestinians, the Jewish love affair with empire – and perhaps the need for empire – is permanent. Jews are therefore rightly labeled by parts of the political Left as privileged. After the Holocaust and with the continuing ambivalence toward Jews, this empire context is perplexing and affects the prophetic. It represents yet another challenge for the Late-Style Jewish Prophetic. For once again Jews remain set apart – with a specific destiny. For after all, if there was no set apart Jewish destiny, the Jewish prophetic would make little, if any, sense. Why reject the protection of power and full inclusion thereof, especially after a history of suffering and struggle, if there isn't a reason beyond the ordinary give and take of life? It is within the context of being set apart and having a destiny that fuels the Jewish prophetic historically and today. It is also what makes the Jewish prophetic so distinctive, so confounding and, sometimes, so irritating to others.

~ 12 ~

Though there is a universal thrust within the Jewish prophetic, the particularity of its cadence and performance is striking. This particularity will continue in the future and become more profound, even and perhaps because of the deepening exile of Jews of Conscience. For the Jewish prophetic has been forced into its final exile within the Jewish world, separated as it is from Constantinian and Progressive Jews, the latter being the helpmate to Constantinian Judaism. While it is difficult to blame Jews for accepting their belated empire security, the Jewish prophetic continues in its specific critique of Jewish empowerment over against another people where it has complete responsibility. The result is an exile from the normative Jewish world for which there will be no return. Shorn of its former distinctive Jewish Diaspora the Jewish prophetic thus enters a different diaspora, what might be called the New Diaspora.

We are always one step ahead
– or behind – the collapse of meaning.

JEWS OF CONSCIENCE IN THE NEW DIASPORA

THE NEW DIASPORA is a global gathering of diverse geographic, cultural, and political exiles. Though these exiles hope to return home in the near future, the reality for most is different. Once displaced always displaced and, world conditions being what they are, the dream of return is for most an illusion. Instead, these exiles, mingling for years and signing with one another that their exile may soon be over, are destined to share their lives with each other. Thus exiles, though often feeling alone and abandoned, actually live in community. This is true for Jews of Conscience, too.

It is the New Diaspora, rather than the Jewish community, where the fate of the Jewish prophetic will be determined. There will be no return to what is considered normative Jewish life. For the Late-Style Jewish Prophetic, Jewishness, always hotly contested, as other particularities also question who is genuinely say Black or feminist and so forth, is fought over by Constantinian and Progressive Jews. The question for the Jewish prophetic in the New Diaspora, however, is how it relates to other exiles and which parts of its particularity it downplays and which parts it emphasizes.

For even in the New Diaspora, where no political, cultural or religious identity dominates and no overall value claims to be the center of the community outside the more universal aspect of the prophetic, the Jewish prophetic is set apart. Part of this has to do with the continuing ambivalence about Jews found even in the New Diaspora and part has to do with the Jewish prophetic continuing to desire and need space for its sustenance and well-being. For in the atmosphere of the New Diaspora that emphasizes the global prophetic, particularity still exists, and not only among Jews.

That Jews are often singled out for their particularity, as if others are free of theirs, is another sign of Jewish vulnerability. Yet, at this point in history, where most Jews live under the protective umbrella of empire, it is difficult for prophetic Jews to argue their prophetic particularity and equally difficult for others who are the victims of empire, where large Jewish populations live, to recognize the prophetic particularity of Jews in their midst.

So it is that the discordant notes of the Late-Style Jewish Prophetic continue to sound. Such a prophetic cannot conform to the Jewish tradition which has disciplined and censored its own indigenous. Nor can the Jewish prophetic simply conform to the prophetic tradition it inherits. Other communities working through their own prophetic, often originally derived or enhanced from their Jewish roots or, better, from the Jewish roots they claim, are on their own journey. Oftentimes they expect the Jewish prophetic to conform to their sense of the prophetic, which, of course, it cannot fully conform to. Though the usual claim of no hierarchy in contemporary discourse that seeks to root out colonialism and imperialism is in play, the reality is that hierarchy exists even when unannounced.

The priorities of other traditions and communities are important. The Jewish prophetic should listen to these claims and acknowledge them. Still, the Jewish prophetic has its own wellbeing and strength to garner; simply bowing to the needs of others, no matter how well intentioned, is hardly enough. Because, even here, in the New Diaspora, the Jewish prophetic remains, among other things, a sign of contradiction. Thus giving over too much on the question of Jewish privilege is neither good for others nor for Jews. A weak Jewish prophetic is in no one's long-term interest. Besides, if history provides any insight, in the long run, the need for Jewish particularity will reassert itself regardless.

The enemy of the Jewish prophetic has been and remains, in its late-style, assimilation. Though the notion of assimilation is typically associated with adopting the norms of the majority cultures Jews traditionally lived within and now, with that assimilation almost complete, with intermarriage, as if marrying

The enemy of the Jewish prophetic has been and remains,
in its late-style, assimilation to unjust power.

Jewish continues the distinctive life of Jews, the deeper element of assimilation is to unjust power.

The prophets in the Hebrew Bible are certain on this matter: the abuse of power within Israel is tantamount to abandoning God or worse, worshipping false Gods. Therefore, in the practice of injustice, Israel is seen as abandoning God's promise and Israel's destiny. The explosion of the Jewish prophetic in a time of post-Holocaust Jewish empowerment signifies that Jews of Conscience, rebelling against the abuse of power in Israel and by Jewish leaders in America and elsewhere, believe that Jews and Jewish history are being prepared for or are already close to a final assimilation.

Jews who left Jewish life for varied reasons over time are now in the media and in the streets, striking Not In Our Name protests for reasons that move beyond the obvious justice issue at hand. Just when their assimilation is almost complete – often denying the distinctiveness of being Jewish – Jews of Conscience highlight their distinctive identity. Interesting, that the Constantinian and Progressive Jews of our time argue that many of these Jews have little Jewish learning or identification and raise the question: In what way are you Jewish?

Yet the primal sense of prophetic Jews, though again rarely articulated in overt Jewish terminology, is their contemporary form of Jewish identification. Attending religious services, studying Jewish texts or joining mainstream Jewish organizations are too often forms of assimilation to venues which purvey injustice.

This lack of learning, distance from Jewish life and overt critique of mainstream Jewishness is maddening to the Jewish establishments wherever they exist. Taken together though and in their diversity, they form a pattern of revolt that informs the Late-Style Jewish Prophetic. From the perspective of the Late-Style Jewish Prophetic, the know-it-alls of Jewish life are engaged in a crime against the Palestinian people which, in turn, is a crime against Jewish history and the Jewish prophetic, the last bastion against the final assimilation of Jews to injustice.

So, yes, the issue is about justice, but not only, for there are many areas of the world where injustice abounds. The concentration by Jews of Conscience on Israel-Palestine is because it has become the primary and final battleground for Jewish history. If this battle for justice is lost the entirety of Jewish history is at stake. Is God also at stake?

The Late-Style Jewish Prophetic makes few, if any, claims about God. Nor is the Late-Style Jewish Prophetic dependent on God, even if God is present without being announced. Such is the indigenous quality of the prophetic in Jewish life. In the same vein, the age-old Jewish argument with God, highlighted once again in the Holocaust and voiced with great depth by Holocaust theologians, recedes as the permanent Israeli occupation of Palestine deepens. Jews of Conscience are wary of any kind of God language because, like certain forms of Jewish affiliation, it often becomes a tool of assimilation to unjust power.

The Late-Style Jewish Prophetic makes few claims about God,
nor is it dependent on God, even if God is present without being announced.

Thus the charade and, for the most part, rejection of Jewish renewal movements, despite the movements' prophetic stance on social and political issues, including Israel-Palestine. The fear is retrenchment, a conservative and traditional swerve in radical clothing. Lurking behind this refusal of assimilation is the adamant rejection of idolatry – the worship of false Gods. Though the worship of false Gods has a history within the prophetic that needs addressing, the possibility of God remains. For in the long run, the prophetic, now independent and on its own, cannot help but ask where the prophetic comes from and how it can be sustained in the New Diaspora. Is it possible to be in an unrelenting and final exile, as prophetic Jews, with others, without God?

The New Diaspora poses further complications for the Jewish prophetic. For in its final exile, its home now in the New Diaspora rather than simply in rebellion against the Jewish mainstream, the Late-Style Jewish Prophetic is returning to internal Jewish issues, Israel-Palestine, for the first time since the Enlightenment and without seeking to return to Jewish life in and of itself. And it is doing so in an overwhelmingly non-Jewish environment that, at times, also concentrates on Israel-Palestine, though with Palestine front and center. Understandably, most non-Jews in the New Diaspora have little, if any, concern for the broader arc of Jewish history. In some ways, then, Jews of Conscience join with others in a prophetic quest for justice, including in Israel-Palestine, with an increasing emphasis on Palestine, but the struggle for one's own history is different than a joint struggle on an issue increasingly invested with international significance.

The New Diaspora includes a broad contingent of Palestinians who, naturally enough, are concerned with their own history rather than Jewish history. Palestine, as a symbol for others, is a boon for Palestinians; no doubt it is problematic as well. This two-edge sword of the internationalization of the Palestine issue is a concern Palestinians will no doubt address. For the Jewish prophetic the focus remains in the context of Jewish history.

Yet how can the fight for Jewish history take place in the New Diaspora? The proper place for such a struggle seems to be within the Jewish community. However, the Jewish community has rejected the Jewish prophetic and exiled its discourse and proponents. Those who remain to fight it out within the Jewish community have trimmed their sails; they argue the edges as the Palestinian people are further displaced and ghettoized. Even the remembrance of the struggle of the Jewish prophetic will find its place in the New Diaspora, a community which does not, indeed, cannot privilege and may not even acknowledge Jewish history as important.

These are preliminary notes on the Late-Style Jewish Prophetic and the New Diaspora. Questions remain on many levels, including its various details and about its future. The challenges by the empire powers against the prophetic and even by its allies for justice will continue and may even accelerate. Worse, over time, the Late-Style Jewish Prophetic might be treated as and may become irrelevant. This possibility must be faced that for a variety of reasons the Jewish prophetic may be in its terminal stage.

Is the Jewish prophetic, Jewish privilege in its essence? Embodying the Jewish prophetic should not be seen as exceptional, for example as the Counsels of Perfection are in the Catholic tradition. There is no hierarchy in Jewish life which relegates embodying the Jewish prophetic to the few and the special. Embodying the prophetic for Jews is normative. That is why the deflection of the prophetic is so strong and why theological systems, such as rabbinic religiosity, and theologies, such as Holocaust theology, are constructed to discipline the prophetic indigenous to Jewish life. This, too, is why the prophetic keeps emerging against the grain and in varied forms even at this late, perhaps last stage.

The danger ahead remains for the Jewish prophetic and for the very concept of Jewishness that roots and carries forth the prophetic to the world. What is the future of Jewish life when the Jewish prophetic is exiled forever and when its memory, in so far as it is remembered, is located not in mainstream Jewish history but within the New Diaspora?

Constantinian Judaism will continue to be recognized by the world as normative Jewishness. Over time, as they already have in the main, Progressive Jews will conform to the protection of empire and, in any meaningful sense, speak less and less about the permanent occupation of Palestine and Palestinians. The allies of Constantinian Jewish life and power will honor this form of Judaism as it conforms to their needs to be recognized as civilized and to salve their conscience. The storehouse of the prophetic, drawn upon in rebellion within and against the mainline Jewish community, might atrophy over time. Like a bank account constantly drawn upon, with few funds added, the future of the Jewish prophetic may be in danger.

So it is. Yet the danger that the Jewish prophetic will atrophy and disappear is hardly new. Who in the world thought that the Holocaust itself would, amid mass death, bring new life to Jews, Jewish and ultimately to the prophetic? A twist of fate, it seems, in the most dramatic, dire and explosive fashions. Who would have thought with all the accomplishments of Jews after the Holocaust, including the creation of the state of Israel that, a few decades later, prophetic Jews of Conscience would cry out against the Jewish abuse of power as the very definition of what it means to be Jewish and as a struggle for Jewish history? For the conspiracy oriented demeanors of Jewish life in Nazi Germany and elsewhere, including in a very different vein, the Jewish establishments in Israel and America, then and now, missed the Jewish rootedness in the prophetic, the indigenous of Jewish life.

Deep in exile, without hope of return, the prophetic,
Jewish and otherwise, breathes deep and free.

THE PROPHETIC WITHOUT GOD OR JUSTICE

DEUTERONOMY, Yom Kippur, Israel the people, Israel the state, Judaism, Jewish, the prophets then, the prophets now, the prophetic community, Constantinian Jews, Progressive Jews, Jews of Conscience, and more. What are Jews to do with all of this?

Even the end of ethical Jewish history, so clear to me, is admittedly up in the air. Will Edward Said, indeed Palestine and the Palestinian people, haunt Jews and Jewish history as a people forever?

The Holocaust and Israel brought Jewish back to the forefront for Jews and for the world. As the years move on, both remain contested. The Holocaust and Israel are now the wellspring of Jewish renewal and Jewish dissent.

What will the future be for Constantinian Judaism and Jews of Conscience? The trajectory seems clear but history is open. Is Yom Kippur that opening or a ritual block against a fundamental change of direction?

The future for Jews cannot be statehood without accountability. Nor can it be the illusion of diaspora. Jews seem stuck in an unfolding history that our religious leaders and intellectuals, indeed our communal life, are unable to free us from to begin anew.

Is Jewish, so important to Jews and others in the world, outside our control? Once a formative event like the Exodus, or Jesus and Muhammad for that matter, becomes a religion, with canonical texts and a religious calendar, over time the individual adherent is, in a sense, swallowed up in a collective. Though individual initiative remains, and conscience, too, the overall power of tradition restricts, even as it can enlighten both. We seem caught in a web of proclamations and promises that surround our being in the world and haunt our interior lives.

Once formative events like the Holocaust and Israel occur, there is no going back. Attempts to do so, even with old fashioned names and texts in new wrappings, exist within the forward thrust that formatives events demand. Neither the Holocaust nor Israel can be transcended; in whatever way they are remembered or represented, they remain. No doubt, other formative events in Jewish history will one day arrive. But formative events are few and far between. The sequential events of Holocaust and the founding of the state of Israel are unique in timeframe and scope.

The Holocaust devastated Jewish life in almost all its prospects. And while Israel seemed for many to be a rescue of Jewish history, in the span of a several decades its militarized manner, accelerating in range and implementation, has turned hope into despair. It is in this context that the Jewish prophetic, once turned outward in an often brilliant way, has turned inward. The turmoil of the Holocaust and Israel has brought the prophetic home.

Yet the returning prophetic is deeply conflicted. Its utopian side has been disciplined. Turned outward, there was little need for the question of God or the communal questioning that often accompanies it. The prophetic coming home forces old questions about God into an arena where God no longer fits. If God could not be called upon in the Holocaust, how can God be called upon in utopian scenarios, especially with their failures? The Jewish prophetic comes home without God and ultimately without hope of a just future.

Can there be a prophetic vision of life without God? To continually invoke images from the Biblical prophets hardly holds forth the ability to believe. At the same time, the secular vision of modernity, itself involving an almost divine belief in progress, has fled the scene. Instead of utopia, the language invoked about the future is more likely to be dystopian. Applying utopic visions within a dystopic framework hardly provides a rallying call for prophetic change in the real world.

Yet the reason utopic visions fall by the wayside, especially when they are amped up, is that human life and the structures that provide for life are decidedly mixed. While I have never rested easy with Richard Rubenstein's sense that history is a cycle of violence and atrocity without end, in the end it is difficult to dispute. This is part of the reason to demur from broad generalities about colonialism and imperialism and their ultimate demise, while recognizing the historical points and genuine hope contained within these formulations.

There has never been a time in history – one doubts there will come a time – when, for any length of years, our earthly life has been or will be free of colonial and imperial power. Thus, prophetic movements which focus almost exclusively on the banishment of these powerful forces, while carrying an important hope forward, are whistling in the dark. Cloaking the prophets in these terms represents a misunderstanding of the prophets and, even if an argument can be made counter to this, a fundamental mistake.

Can the prophetic be invoked in a context where a dystopian reality is assumed for a future without the possibility that the invocation of the prophetic will bring a reversal of situation of injustice at hand? Already stripped of God as the bulwark of the prophetic, at least as a public claim, is it possible for the prophetic to survive if stripped of its utopic promise?

At the outset the stripping of the utopic seems easier than the proclamation of God's presence. Yet in much prophetic speech and action today, the invocation of God already seems rhetorical. The next step, shedding the utopic promise, seems more difficult, since without this sensibility what is the justice struggle about?

Are the prophets God's mirror image. Of defeat?

Of course, justice must be pursued relentlessly. But justice, more justice than is present, will, for the most part, be found on the margins. For people in need, the vast majority of humanity, these margins are crucial; for many the margins of justice mean the difference between life and death. Unfortunately, justice wholesale, if momentarily achieved, and justice on the margins, the more likely victory, is too often reversed in short order or, in due time, will be redistributed in an unequal manner. The balance between justice and injustice is inherently unstable. Sometimes it seems that those calling for global justice are like those who once called on an all-powerful God. Such calls are questions of faith not politics.

In the 1980s, a Catholic priest from Spain, Joan Casañas, published a fascinating and provocative essay about the Chilean guerrilla fighters in their struggle against the Pinochet dictatorship. Traveling with these fighters, Casañas queried them about their belief in God or lack thereof. What he found with them and others lacking justice in Latin America is that many had grave doubts about God, even as they put their life on the line for justice. Moreover, they were unable to accept a conception of God without justice. This prompted Casañas to posit that belief in and speech about God is impossible without justice achieved. Only in a just society does God make sense.

Casañas proposes a limit on speech about God – until justice is in place. But Casañas leaves to the side the difficulty, if not impossibility, of justice being achieved over time in one society, let alone a number of societies and ultimately existing globally. For example, if justice is achieved in Chile but not Argentina, can God be proclaimed in one nation but not the other?

While Casañas's understanding of God and justice is provocative on many levels, posing an incredibly deep reckoning with God, the God question he leaves on the table is even more provocative. Since justice in one society is so difficult to imagine, let alone achieve, and justice on a global scale a virtual impossibility, Casañas opens the door to the possibility that our belief in God in general and across religions will be silenced forever.

Where can the prophetic go, if not from God and without justice achieved or, at least on the way? Is the prophetic to be left with a creedal affirmation similar to the Christian belief in the return of Jesus, now unfulfilled for thousands of years and counting? The charge of God as pie in the sky, so often invoked, might be applied to prophetic hope. Can prophetic hope be held accountable for what seems to be an indefinite, perhaps eternal, delay of justice?

Perhaps even more difficult to accept is the possibility that the prophetic, like the prophets, not only failed to achieve the justice they spoke about and acted within but that the prophetic, with its many-sided call, cannot achieve its calling. The prophets and the prophetic may be essential to conscience and a deep spiritual life but its hallmark, justice achieved, is not one of them.

What are the prophets about if not justice? And if they are about justice and justice will not be attained, are the prophets then consigned to the category of aspirational symbols of what would be important to but will never be achieved? If so, the prophets become like God, a matter of belief.

Some would ask, and importantly so, if we take this route without God or justice, what will prompt us to struggle for a better world. Contemporary radical theology seems poised at that precipice: neither fully believing in God or the fulfillment of justice but feeling it necessary to keep the symbolic architecture of both. This begs the question of the next generation that does not grow up with the certainty that their parents felt failing but kept up the appearance for others, and even for the parents need to deflect from themselves the conclusion their children might arrive at. Here we have the propping up of faith and identity lest the alternative, a collapse, take root.

Collapse or a deeper reckoning? Sometimes we have to take stock, even a fall, in order to establish a new balance. For among Jews and others of conscience, justice has assumed the place of God in their theological proclamations. And though both God and justice will remain in the theological mix, no matter how much neither are enough, separately or together. Nor is this to suggest the need to look for suitable replacements. If we are honest with ourselves, without public proclamations of God or justice we have reached another ending without an apparent beginning. The way is through, not back or ahead.

Is there a way of moving with and through God and justice without proclaiming either? At our juncture in history, it seems best to understand the limits of both through what might be called a dystopian solidarity. A few years ago, I explored dystopian solidarity as the "embrace of the prophetic tradition come alive, in its deconstruction and in its committed waywardness, visible wailing, and solitude." To this should be added the New Diaspora as the location for this solidarity, and as the place where this deconstruction, waywardness, wailing and solitude find a home or at least a place to find its always evolving voice.

Perhaps we are left here, in a shortened conclusion worth a lifetime of journey and reflection – that what is available to us are only fragments of justice and fragments of God and that to go beyond either is too much, adopting a messianic vision we know to be inadequate and fragmented, if it appears at all. What is a faith we know the moment it is proclaimed to be false? And especially among the privileged, who does such a faith serve?

Some years ago the Jewish Holocaust poet, Paul Celan, began a poem – "The world is gone, I must carry you." Paraphrasing Celan in relation to the Late-Style Jewish Prophetic and the late style in other traditions, we might say – "The world is gone, we must carry each other." The interplay here is one of solitude and solidarity. Yet even here a deflection might be in order. If the world is gone, do we really carry one another outside our rhetoric?

A further challenge comes into view: Is the prophetic the way the Jewish tradition parses this solitude/solidarity divide? Does the prophetic close down the reality of our broken world and essential aloneness by joining both in the prophetic journey, albeit without a conclusive end? In this journey postulating that, nevertheless and despite the odds, there is meaning in an apparently meaningless world?

The prophetic thrives in its strength and partly in its contradictions.

GUARDING THE PROPHETIC

WHAT DOES a Jew of Conscience, indeed a person of conscience, do when the future arrives in one's lifetime? We are inundated with the idea of future shock but, for the most part, that shock, if we pay attention, is already here.

There are many levels and arenas to this future arrived but in the case of Jews it is particularly striking. The shift in the center of the Jewish world is just one example, though a major one. More or less, in our lifetimes, the center of the Jewish world has shifted from Europe to America and Israel. The forcible uprooting of Jews was extreme: the shift in Jewish geography, discourse and activity is as well.

In less than one hundred years and accelerating in the last eighty years, Jews went from a rooted but scattered diaspora population, within and outside non-Jewish empire configurations, without empowerment, a state or military, to a concentrated population in America and Israel, thus protected by a world and regional superpower. In this shift, Jewish rhetoric and ritual, uprooted and empowered, has assumed an empire cadence. Where only recently Jews were down and vulnerable, Jews are now up and protected. To say that the material life of a majority of Jews has undergone a sea change is an understatement.

There may be more ahead. What if a positive direction takes place and the occupation and oppression of Palestinians come to an end? What would a one-state secular democracy in Israel-Palestine mean for Jewish life, for Jews of Conscience, for the Jewish prophetic?

Just as Jews of Conscience rarely address in a serious manner their empire benefits or, if they do discuss them, even fervently, few relinquish those benefits, so, too, the deeper reasons for their reengagement with Jewish life vis-a-vis dissent on Israel's abuse of power, is mostly left undiscussed. The Holocaust and Israel brought a renewed commitment to the Jewish world. Would justice for Palestinians – the diminution of Jewish power and vulnerability – return the long-term Jewish trends of disengagement from Jewish life?

Justice for Palestinians is an imperative in and of itself but its ramifications for Jewish life, Jews of Conscience and the prophetic should not be ignored. For, consciously or not, in terms of commitment to Jewish life, it may be that the status quo on both sides of the Jewish civil war needs the stalemate in Israel-Palestine to continue.

Beyond intentions, here I think of how formative events and their ability to orient, disorient and reorient a community's life and individual commitments. There are more than a few Jewish thinkers who have pointed to the memory of the Holocaust and support for Israel as having taken on religious significance for Jews around the world. It is also true that support for Palestinian freedom has become a formative event for dissenting Jews. In both sensibilities, God is relegated to a peripheral role, if God is even part of the picture. The terrain of the Jewish civil war is worldly; it is primarily about Jewish identity. We know what Jewish identity looks like today. What would it look like if the formative event of Palestinian freedom became a reality?

True, the prophetic moment cannot be held hostage by a projected outcome, if indeed a just resolution came to fruition. Yet often as not, even with significant positive changes in the offing, the victory lap in reach is often truncated by the reality of the change itself. If it is true that exiles around the world rarely return home and, even if they do physically, the change around them and within them is too much for a true homecoming to occur, the Jewish condition of exile is no exception. Once an exile always an exile. As well, justice after injustice is never a return or an end in itself. There will always be injustice, even among those who right a wrong. Dissent will always be necessary, especially as the reality of victory sets in.

Victory is important and ephemeral – when one justice front recedes another comes into view. In the case of the contemporary Jewish situation, the very empowerment that Jews needed after the Holocaust, and achieved in Israel and America in ways unforeseen and certainly, in such a short time, has to be judged as incredible. This very success has been, in another way, at least from the perspective of Jews of Conscience, a disaster. Jews of Conscience are employing the same energy that built Jewish empowerment to deconstruct it.

Would Jews be better off if this deconstruction was successful? Functionally, empowerment has, in a material and psychological sense, freed Jews of Conscience to cry out against the injustice of parts of that empowerment, certainly with regard to Palestinians. Yet today the critique of Jewish empowerment has grown wider under the rubric of white privilege and colonialism. The particular critique regarding Israel is constantly expanding. The emphasis among Jews of Conscience now is on an intersectional solidarity across racial, ethnic and gender lines. In this scenario, at least in the United States, the Jewish hope to be in solidarity with others who are denied rights and who are suffering exclusion and more comes at the cost of being identified as part of the broader Jewish community that itself is part, and depending on how responsibility is parsed, perhaps a major part of the problem. In short, the Jewish civil war is only partly in relation to Palestinians. For Jews of Conscience this involves the global structure of the empowered few against the disempowered many.

Jews of Conscience, embodying their presence in the New Diaspora, are joining forces with those on the side of justice regardless of their origins and communal affiliations. Yet the question remains: Is this promised cross-affiliation an equal playing field? Regardless of intention, history plays its role and the singled-out reality of Jews historically and today continues.

The prophet's monastery is the world.

Though the commitment of Jews of Conscience often rightly draws admiration from many, the double edge of historic anti-Jewish stereotypes, spoken and unspoken, continue. Jews of Conscience remain in-between the empowered Jewish community *and* on the outer dimensions of global, national and local life. Thus, the prophetic enters a quite different arena than in its previous incarnations, with hands stretched outward in solidarity while embattled internally in the Jewish civil war.

The Biblical prophets were often caught in-between though in a different way, with God's backing, calling out Israel's sins of injustice within while at times, again with God's backing, on Israel's enemies to deliver a revengeful blow. Jews of Conscience in their prophetic mode are looking for a systemic disempowering of the powerful, in Israel for Jews, in America for a broader community, including the Jewish elite. Yet again, the in-between quality of Jewish life intervenes, since the in-between sense of Jews of Conscience is, to some extent, stabilized by Jewish empowerment. What if that stabilizing force was destabilized, if everything, indeed, was turned inside out? Would the Jewish prophetic, now on different foundational grounds, strike as hard as it does now?

The Christian pretense of universality is, on the one hand, false, and on the other hand, its least attractive quality. Are Jews of Conscience, albeit from a different history and demography, beginning to travel in that universalist direction? The prophetic arrived and has been sustained partly at least through its containment, its partiality, and its undivided focus. Within the fiery confines of an enclosed particularity, the prophetic has struggled to find its voice. This containment – confinement – accounts for the prophetic's boldness and its exile. In the intersectional application of the prophetic, especially in the New Diaspora, will the Jewish prophetic, now shared across communities and traditions, lose its edge? Other communities have their own prophetic, often first glimpsed or inspired by them within the Jewish fold, though interpreted through their own particular lens. With the need of Jews of Conscience to be aware and give space to the consideration of other views and cadences, lose the distinctiveness of the Jewish indigenous?

Looked from another vantage point, since the prophetic is always contextual and negotiated, perhaps Jews of Conscience, even in their broadening, are doing something they are unaware of – guarding the prophetic. Perhaps subconsciously they see the prophetic in Jewish life slipping away. Just as support for Palestinian freedom is for Jews of Conscience an attempt to keep Jews and the Jewish tradition from fully assimilating to injustice, perhaps the broadening of the prophetic is their way of safeguarding the prophetic from disappearing completely. Thus, the world to come, the utopic sensibility of many Jews of Conscience, may be less about belief in overcoming injustice than it is to safeguard the prophetic.

Could safeguarding the Jewish prophetic be the essential thrust of Jewish history through times of tribulation and power, with the knowledge that somehow, the prophetic, even in its evident disappointment and dismissal, must remain? Guarding the prophetic seems defensive, especially in our liberal idea of accepting and promoting openness and diversity, but every community has its own way of guarding its core, however defined, through times of segregation and integration, powerlessness and power. In the guarding of cultural, political and religious communal cores, are other communities more or less like Jews, making Jewish distinctiveness, in the broader sense, less distinctive? The persistence of the prophetic, even by stretching it far from the particularity which is its strength may be a way of protecting the prophetic from its invocation as an enabler of unjust power.

The question remains as to the possibility of the prophetic's recovery from injustices that seem permanent. Jews of Conscience may then face a time when the prophetic becomes unrecognizable to itself. If so, what future formative event in Jewish history could occur that would signal a broad recognition among Jews that without the prophetic and the communal ascent among the primary carrier of the prophetic in history to the prophetic's primacy, that Jewish and human history will be hollowed out of meaning?

The world will never be run in a prophetic mode. The politics of the prophetic in our world couldn't be farther from implementation. In the very broadening of the prophetic, it can be argued that the prophetic among Jews of Conscience is becoming less and less political, rendering their prophetic invocation as a surrender. The prophetic remains, at least for now, a process, a negotiation, a stance from which to imagine a different world. However, the warning is clear: there may come a time when the prophetic enters an exile from which there is no return.

The prophet carries a people's history, judging it with a hope and compassion that compels us.

LIKE A DEATH SENTENCE – WITH ASSURANCE

IT IS AUGUST, a year since I began my Yom Kippur journal and encountered, once again, the long gone yet quite present Edward Said. The world remains mostly as it was last year – at least the news reports say so. It is a year since the United States left Afghanistan. Gaza remains in lockdown and Israel's periodic bombing of Gaza continues. India is celebrating its birth as a nation but the mourning over partition, and its resultant human casualties and massive dislocation, remains.

In August, too, the novelist, Salmon Rushdie, was attacked within inches of his life. Rushdie planned to discuss the need for artistic freedom; the lingering religious decree, now downplayed by Iran, obviously outlasts its initial passion. And, yes, the new evidence of iceberg melting points to an underestimation by scientists of the tremendous environmental damage already began.

The news cycle has more, much more. The details change and, from a longer view, remain more or less the same. So much for the prophetic warnings and interruptions traversing our troubled world. Negotiation with power seems one-sided.

Did I leave out the war in Ukraine? The Supreme Court's decision voiding the constitutional right to abortion? The FBI's search and retrieval of Top Secret documents from Donald Trump's Florida country club, Mar-a-Lago?

When I first started writing books, editors encouraged me to place my narrative outside any particular timeframe, lest the news of the day and the writing become dated. Today, though, timelessness is timely. The faster the pace the more repetitive things become. As time passes, the author and reader is called upon to fill in the blanks.

I am at home having just turn seventy years of age. I was looking through my manuscript hunting for misspellings and wobbly syntax, when Zooming Torah study, it dawned on me that Yom Kippur – "the day without a future," I wrote of years ago – is turning the religious calendar corner again and heading straight at us – at me. Had I forgotten the yearly religious cycle? Did I think my writing last year had set Yom Kippur in stone?

I am violating my "preface first" admonition by writing an epilogue after the preface. It seems that once I get going more thoughts come my way and, sometimes, I keep things open ended, even when I rhetorically close things down. Even at seventy, life is a continuing discussion, a series of encounters, which has an afterlife when alive and sometimes even after individuals depart life for parts unknown.

A friend once remarked after reading a book of mine that she experienced my writing "like a death sentence – with assurance." I have pondered this response often wondering what this might say about me and to me. As I enter my eighth decade I turn that aphorism over again.

When I consider what I leave behind, my legacy, I also ponder what we leave behind, our legacy. Since our lives and witness cannot be the end of things. Nor can they be a Hallmark greeting card hope. There are too many doomsayers and yes men and women to join that crowd.

If I assert that Jewish is fated, for example, and that the prophetic persists, but is on its last legs, do I honor those who have struggled for a better world and those who struggle today? Or do I betray them? If I cannot join the chorus of "We Shall Overcome," and stand apart, do I assert I have a higher standard and a more fervent sense of justice than others?

Personality and our life journey are individual markers. To a large extent, though, both are shaped by the community we come from, by the tradition we inherit and by the history we live within. The individual without the collective is an illusion. So, too, is the sense that the collective is all.

What to do with the trauma associated with our journeys and how these traumas shape and reshape us? Trauma is individual and collective. Sometimes the individual and the collective can move with and through trauma and, through time and struggle, form a new wholeness. Other individuals and collectives may be shattered by trauma without renewal. Left behind with both, at the end, are fragments – to be silenced or shared.

Can we be grateful for the trauma, the shattering and the struggle, sometimes won and other times lost, for wholeness? Decades ago, I remember dividing *Practicing Exile* into three sections – Exile, Traveling the Diaspora and Gratitude. The first sections of the book flowed easily but when I came to gratitude, the terrain became more difficult. How can I be grateful for a journey of such little success and with so many bumps in the road?

At seventy, I return to the theme of gratitude. What greater gift than to embody, in however limited and flawed way, with others, the indigenous of one's community? With a large impact, in victory, our journey would be an obvious triumph. In defeat, one that continues and increases, our evaluation is up for grabs. Either way, gratitude is hard to describe let alone experience.

Is fidelity in defeat an illusion? Suffering as a sign of fidelity is certain in some Christian circles where loss and suffering are seen as redemptive, less so in the Jewish tradition that emphasizes doing without reward. Yet the question remains whether fidelity is real without taking on suffering when it is unavoidable.

Hiding is the way of many, in Jewish circles, yes, and among progressives in other traditions too. I think of those who hold fast rhetorically for solidarity with Jews but, out of fear of reprisal from the larger Jewish community, turn their back on Jews of Conscience. How often I experienced this firsthand, especially in the academy, when liberationists of all stripes seek to build their specialized empires and fear taking on Jewish dissidents. One asks about these empire builders: What are they really about?

Jews of Conscience, while reaching out to others, often face turned backs when an embodied and courageous solidarity is needed. Jews of Conscience know firsthand that the bond of solidarity has a slippery slope quality to it when it comes to Israel-Palestine. Yet the demand of Jewish solidarity across racial and gender lines is demanded by others regardless. Forced into an exile within exile, what are Jews of Conscience to do?

The only way to be prophetic is to embody the prophetic. Embodying the prophetic means, rather than hope, whether in victory or defeat, and often somewhere in the middle of both, that something important is at stake. Could the measure of success be the embodiment of the prophetic itself? This may be the assurance my friend found, that even in an exile that has no end, there are those who say: "Nevertheless, this is where I stand."

If the prophet and the prophetic embody a death sentence *and* assurance for others, do they also embody both for the individual who embodies the prophetic? If the prophetic is a witness to others of loss and fidelity, becoming a witness to others that there are markers in our world worthy of commitment that can or does cause suffering, is the embodied prophetic also a witness to those who embody the prophetic?

Often those who embody the prophetic think that embodiment is a one way street; performing the prophetic for others what is at stake with little in return. For the prophetic, always in public, is a performance within traditions that have developed a cadence and ritual that calls attention to the prophetic itself. Yet, over time, performing the prophetic, if mostly or only for others, can become a rote performance, an empty actor whose being is as predictable as a Sunday sermon.

Perhaps that is the reason for the prophetic to periodically deconstruct its own performance and tradition. Hence the Late-Style Jewish Prophetic may need invocation before the end or at different ends, in whatever time period it lives through. The prophetic must be up to the task it specifically lives and breathes within. Context within essence is the continual challenge for the prophetic.

But much of this is to get ahead of the prophetic itself, as if the Jewish indigenous is a big deal. While this can be the case, in fact, the prophetic should be part of ordinary Jewish life in large and small details. The prophetic only becomes extraordinary in times of crisis when the ordinary ethical flow of Jewish life, proposed as the norm, is upset to such a point that the Jewish stakes are raised to an emergency level.

What happens when that emergency seems to be and may be without end? What if the emergency, like Israel's occupation of Palestine and the Jewish entanglement with empire, is permanent? What is the prophetic to do, what will the prophetic become, if there is no way back to the ordinary flow of Jewish life?

All prophetic writing of depth,
whatever power it contains, is about loss.

This may have been the case in Biblical times if indeed a modern form of history could be applied to the past. Was the future return, spoken of in the prophetic literature, in reality, a fantasy in real time or retrofitted for the listening and now reading Bible audience? Perhaps this is one of the reasons the rabbis of ancient times kept alive Torah literature but encased it in Halacha wrapping. The rabbis hoped that Jewish teaching and law could keep the reality of injustice and the possibility of return on an even keel.

The instability of the prophetic. Can this be embraced as a form of assurance? Strange assurance it is, if this be the case. The assurance that through it all, the prophetic, tamped down, even by the rabbis, and other religious authorities, survives.

The survival of the prophetic is one thing. Yet the survival of the individual is another. What happens within the person who embodies the prophetic? The prophetic exterior itself, as a symbol and a witness, plays its part but the interior of the embodied prophetic – what is within – is another matter.

Joan Casañas writes of the interior of the freedom fighter in Chile and beyond as participating in the task of making God exist. In the meantime of injustice, where God cannot be claimed, what do freedom fighters experience? In Casañas's terms, at least at moments, they experience an "elucidation through abundance," where the "reality of their struggle, in one of its many aspects, with such solidity and fullness, with an overflowing brilliance and with such absoluteness, that they spontaneously, poetically, and more than poetically – with the simplicity of children, but with the force of adults – divulge the reality that they are experiencing." Casañas reports that this elucidation through abundance is "both speakable and unspeakable; the much and the more than much; abundance glimpsed from this angle and that: the historical and what goes beyond it; the unpredictable that may be a reality tomorrow; the human and what exceeds that which we grasp as human; the whole and even more; the horizon that attracts us along the way and the far side of that horizon, brighter still."

Casañas brings to light the mystical component of commitment to justice among those brought up in a Christian-infused culture that, through violence, overlaid indigenous spirituality. There were occasions when the Biblical prophets had such visions. But the Jewish prophetic, then and even more so now, has dimensions within its mystical component that interrupts it. The interruption is the prophets mourning the loss of God's promise, of an exceptionalism squandered, of an unrelenting exile after confrontation with power and the sense that what was to be, if it ever existed, won't be put together again. The Late-Style Jewish Prophetic, in its further deconstruction, adds another layer to this mourning – the collapse of the original promise, as if what was fated from the beginning will be played out endlessly. Mourning the mourning?

We think of embodying the prophetic as a positive affirmation, even an honor. Is it also, perhaps even primarily, a form of mourning?

It is difficult to think of mourning as assurance. This may be another reason that even in the New Diaspora, Jews are set apart. As well, mourning may serve as a protection of the prophetic, now widely embraced and claimed by fellow travelers in the New Diaspora, as primarily originating and carried by Jews.

Over the years, I have come to think of the prophets as light gatherers – in the darkness. Can one in mourning, those in mourning, be gatherers of light? A strange juxtaposition it seems at first glance. Yet another Jewish distinctive.

Gathering light, for the prophets, in the darkness of mourning, exile it is, while continuing on. Holding history and the present, the end and a beginning together, is the kind of depth needed, with others, lest the light found alone or together become superficial. This may be the Jewish contribution to the New Diaspora; a disciplined encounter of the indigenous prophetic, honed by tradition, quite old and, within deconstruction, ever new.

The assurance side of the death sentence might be found here. History is a movement that cannot continue without past and present being fused in a dynamic reckoning. That reckoning produces, albeit one step at a time, the possibility of a future that is more attentive, more focused and (possibly) more just. "More" is shadowed and limited, true, but perhaps realistically attuned to the possible, halting the tendency to mystify the worldly reality of vying interests, competing powers and dividing imperialisms, while maintaining the solitary and collective cries of suffering humanity.

The prophetic is not the prime mover in our world. Rather the prophetic is a consistent negotiation. The negotiation is less the much criticized option of a third way and rather a different path that appears, disappears and reappears in and out of time. The prophetic negotiation is hard-edged and insistent, calling power to change its way. The prophetic negotiation appeals to the real and demands the fulfillment of its own rhetoric of being of and for the people. The prophetic fails and continues on.

The prophetic lives and breathes in the danger zone; solidarity in negotiation with power becomes a target. Another danger, though, is the deflection that comes with group identification. As if one's stance for justice alone, now shared with others, is mission accomplished or about to be. What is missing in the group, at least as articulated, is the aloneness of the prophetic voice.

The movement from prophet to prophetic is telling, for the prophet stands apart. Too often today the prophetic movement looks askance at anyone assuming the prophet mantle. Usually couched in tones of hierarchy, the underlying fear of that singular voice represents the vulnerability that comes with the territory. So here the prophetic community, in its role as guarding the prophetic, may also deflect that voice, if not undermine it substantially.

Without the deepest solitude and the fear found there, with the possibility that everything has become undone, part of the prophetic voice, so essential, is lost. Insistence without loss becomes cheerleading without consequence.

Could it be that by embracing the prophetic, we deflect it?

Deflection has many sides, no doubt, and we cannot pretend that others carry forth delusions without interrogating our own. The reduction of cognitive dissonance crosses all sorts of boundaries. Yet this prophetic gamble, without gain and against the tide, rendering us exiles, is a longstanding one, anciently held and present today, against all reasonable odds, by those Jews who seek to draw near, to embrace and to embody the prophetic.

How late it is to hold high the prophetic, some may note, and correctly so. Surely too late to salvage what has been squandered. Still, the miracle it seems is that prophetic force in Jewish life remains so strong that Jews of Conscience are making the statement of statements; that without an ethics outside and within empowerment, Jewish cannot exist as a normative force but only in an exile that sees no future beyond its own embodiment.

Epilogue

The only reason to be Jewish today is to draw near, to embrace, and to embody the prophetic – all the rest is commentary.

MY JUDGMENT DAY

SO IT WENT.

A year after, to the day, of my previous experience of Yom Kippur.

Instead of Zooming into Tzedek Chicago for the end of the Days of Awe, I spent Yom Kippur in a huge medical center, seemingly a city block in length and width. Like the churches I first encountered in the Deep South. I thought then and on Yom Kippur this year: What in God's name goes on here?

The Yom Kippur/medical conflation was unfortunate and unavoidable; time constraints abounded, my neurologist was departing and friendly companions were available to drive and accompany me.

What's a Jew of Conscience to do?

On the other hand, it might have been the right venue for whatever judgment came my way. On the Big Day.

Judgment in our modern world comes primarily through the technology we thrive and despair within.

My Yom Kippur liturgical experience was a SPECT scan, a marvel of a machine, that gathers images of the striatum which facilitates the transportation of dopamine. After the DaTscan, the radioactive tracer for dopamine transporters, is injected, it circulates through the brain. For thirty minutes the SPECT scan gathers images of the striatum, measuring the dopamine contained there. The testing indicates the loss of dopamine-containing nerve cells within the brain and points toward or away from a Parkinson's determination.

Lying down for thirty minutes in the SPECT scan was painful on my neck in the extreme. I didn't know if I could make it through. I was determined to do it, however; I needed a final confirmation of the suspected Parkinson's. Accompanying the pain and the duration was a whirring background noise and voices alerting me to the timing left. When the SPECT scan was over, I was relieved to put it mildly.

I experienced my time in the SPECT scan as a dystopian eternity. It felt like I had been transported into a different universe. The sounds of the SPECT scan and the voices I heard came to me like mystical voices from parts unknown. A religious experience of sorts. What to make of it remains a question.

The day after I spoke by phone to my departing neurologist and he finally confirmed what we had suspected all along. Parkinson's it is, though, fortunate for me, it's early onset and arrived late in my life.

Nonetheless Judgment Day had arrived.

I took the news well. I queried my neurologist about the long-range effects on my health and life. If all goes according to plan, it seems I have ten years or so left of reasonable life. There are variables that cannot be mapped in advance. So depending on this and that, before everything more or less collapses, life continues on.

This means I have time to walk the beach and paint. And time to write whatever is left inside me.

Timelines are important. For our individual and collective judgement dates and our journey after.

Is it better to know in advance when our time is up? We all live under death sentences. With assurance?

My father had Parkinson's. I know what happens. Over time. All things must pass. Away.

There we have it. I missed Tzedek's Yom Kippur service but am receiving Rabbi Rosen's sermons he preached via Facebook.

The first sermon I received is on Shabbat. As an alternative way of life. Individually and collectively. Traditional it is, though with an updated justice twist. I will read it again as Shabbat in the present arrives. The second sermon carries the title: "Living a Judaism Beyond Zionism." This sermon is mostly about the benefits of developing another take on Diaspora Judaism.

I do observe Shabbat but am doubtful about its communal application. Since I am not a Diaspora Jew I can only read it as an observer.

I continue to think there's no way back or around our present impasse. I'm dubious about reinvigorating ancient rituals or observances as wholistic venues. On Judaism and Israel I believe the question is about Israel, the state and how it will be transformed or not, not about Zionism however defined, and how Israel relates to Jewish not Judaism.

Is Judaism a religion? An often unasked question whose answer is simply assumed. Whether we wash our hands of Israel in our religiosity, Israel as a state will continue on. The great majority of Jews of Conscience are engaged or re-engaged with Jewish because of Israel's abuse of power, not for the promise of the end of Israel or the future of Judaism.

But that is to get ahead – or behind – our individual judgment days, Yom Kippur notwithstanding, and our individual fate in light of history.

A few years ago my younger son reflecting on my life, wrote: "To make a future, to make it an object and work on it, is often not possible within the prophetic frame. It is the prophetic call to think beginnings without a future."

I have thought about his insight into the prophetic often, without being able to get to the essence of its meaning. But pondering his words anew after my SPECT Scan Judgment Day, a new possibility emerges.

Why not, in the days ahead – while I still have legs to walk and the ability to breathe easily – simply go my way and let history have the final say, especially since I doubt any of our visions will win the day. Then we would have the present, perhaps as a blessing and with a new-found freedom, to pursue our fidelity without being bound to the past or to the future, neither of which we can make or control.

It may be that the prophetic frame at the end is our beginning. Yet another chance to begin again.

Beginning, beginning, beginning? Do our ends justify our beginnings?

Fidelity as our many beginnings.

Yet beginnings without destinations aren't for the faint of heart. Why begin over and over again if there's no end in sight?

This is our fate it seems, even if destinations are only in our minds. It may be that beginnings are what we have. Why not affirm what we have and leave the imagined end in other hands?

I think of the traditional Jewish prayer of rising from sleep, now without God or justice. Thanking God simply for another day. The practice of exile writ large and small comes into view.

What does all of this mean for our Yom Kippur confessions and repentance? I haven't mused much on repentance and for a specific reason: In a world without God or justice it seems that both become symbolic markers, of modified importance, without collective power and effect. This doesn't mean that confession and repentance are – only – hypocrisies. It does mean that those in need can only hope that more, much more, is on the way. But without expectation, those on the other side of history will mostly remain where they are or be replaced by others.

Where individual and collective conscience ends, do they begin again? If conscience ends and begins again, does conscience ultimately reside within or come from Somewhere Else?

Can conscience function without a referent outside itself, even if that referent is argued with, disputed or denied?

Can encounters be that referent if something in history is at stake?

Can history be at stake if there are no ends, only beginnings? Like the religious calendar, linearity has its limits. Yet without ends, we feel adrift. Why bother, indeed take on suffering, if so little, or nothing, is achievable?

In these last Yom Kippurs, Edward Said and my own fate have been my primary encounters. History and my individual fate have been at stake. But in a broader sense, they were – are – connected.

And so, in a sense, the judgment – ours – is announced.

Are we powerless to intervene as the judgment is announced?

Encounters may be our power. Keeping the lines open, even as limitations are imposed. Perhaps we are engaged in a Sisyphean enterprise as Albert Camus envisioned the Greek myth of consciousness within constraints. With Camus, we are free, within our limits, to begin again. While being bound determines our need for strength and endurance.

Am I bound to a God who can no longer be announced in public, as a claim, that others should attend to? To a history of ethics and struggle that has come to an end in our lifetime? To a religion that, even with revision, repeats what has been asserted in different eras but never within the empire configurations that most Jews live and prosper within today?

For this I remain certain: Without the prophetic there is no meaning in history; There may be no meaning in history; The prophet embodies the possibility of meaning – and God – in history.

Does such a prophetic – and prophet – represent our possibility – and our beginning?

Now in its late-style incarnation, deconstructed and fragmented, the prophetic must carry its indigenous force with confidence. That nevertheless there is meaning in history and in our individual lives.

Can the Late-Style Jewish Prophetic continue gathering light in this darkness?

If we think ends, it is doubtful. If we think beginnings, what we see when we look around, is. The Jewish prophetic is all around us, in great diversity, and perhaps this is so precisely because Jewish history, at least as a carrier of ethics, has reached an end.

There we are – I am. With judgment in place. Beginning again.

Marc Ellis

Edward Said